CW00555927

CONSERVATIVE REALISM

CONSERVATIVE REALISM

NEW ESSAYS ON CONSERVATISM

EDITED BY
Kenneth Minogue

HarperCollins*Publishers*

IN ASSOCIATION WITH
THE CENTRE FOR POLICY STUDIES

HarperCollins*Publishers*
77–85 Fulham Palace Road,
Hammersmith, London W6 8JB

First published by HarperCollins*Publishers* 1996
1 3 5 7 9 8 6 4 2

ISBN 0 00 255769 X

Set in Linotype Janson by
Rowland Phototypesetting Ltd,
Bury St Edmunds, Suffolk

Printed and bound in Great Britain by
Caledonian International Book Manufacturing Ltd, Glasgow

Contents

PREFACE BY KENNETH MINOGUE vii
CONTRIBUTORS ix
FOREWORD BY BARONESS THATCHER xiii

INTRODUCTION: On Conservative Realism 1
Kenneth Minogue

I America's 'Exceptional Conservatism' 9
Irving Kristol

II Conservatism and Cultural Identity 23
John O'Sullivan

III Conservative Realism and Christian Democracy 44
Noel Malcolm

IV The Perils of Principle 68
Richard Griffiths

V The Free Market and Civic Conservatism 80
David Willetts MP

VI Conservative Realism: The Disposition of Sceptical Faith 98
Timothy Fuller

VII Whose is This Image and Superscription? Money and Sovereignty 112
Ray Evans

VIII Unrealism and Foreign Policy: Russia and the Middle East 129
David Pryce-Jones

IX Does Realism Have a Future? 138
Owen Harries

X Three Conservative Realists 154
Kenneth Minogue

APPENDIX: British Conservatism in the 1990s 173
Shirley Letwin

INDEX 181

Preface

THE FOLLOWING ESSAYS by writers from Britain, America and Australia began their lives at a Conference at Cumberland Lodge in Windsor Great Park in April 1995. Their formal inspiration was the work of three notable conservative philosophers: Michael Oakeshott, Elie Kedourie and Shirley Letwin, but the authors were left entirely free to reflect on the current situation of conservatism. At the dinner which inaugurated the conference, we were delighted to entertain Sir Denis and Lady Thatcher, and even more pleased that she agreed that the remarks she made on that occasion could become a foreword to the volume. Lady Thatcher must not, of course, be held to any of the opinions expressed in the essays, nor indeed will the authors themselves be found to agree with each other. The real coherence of the volume lies in the pleasures of sharing in an exploration of political reality from a conservative point of view. The Centre for Policy Studies sponsored the enterprise, and I am grateful to those who provided the finance for it: Rupert Murdoch and HarperCollins, Lord Pearson of Rannoch, the Bradley and Olin Foundations and the CPS itself. My greatest debt of gratitude is to Gerry Frost, who as Director of the CPS smoothed out every difficulty.

Kenneth Minogue

Contributors

RAY EVANS has been Executive Officer at the Western Mining Corporation in Melbourne since 1982. Previously, he taught electrical engineering at Deacon University in Geelong. He is president of the H. R. Nicholls Society, and has written extensively on environmentalism, the movements of indigenous peoples and social and political issues affecting industry.

PROFESSOR TIMOTHY FULLER is Professor of Political Science and Dean of the College at Colorado College, Colorado Springs. He has written extensively on political philosophy, and has edited a new expanded edition of Michael Oakeshott's *Rationalism in Politics*. He has also edited so far three volumes of both published and unpublished writings of Oakeshott, and *The Politics of Faith and the Politics of Scepticism* appeared in Spring 1996.

PROFESSOR RICHARD GRIFFITH has been Professor of French at King's College London since 1990, having taught previously at Oxford, Cambridge and Cardiff. He has written, among other books, a biography of Marshal Pétain and more recently *The Use of Abuse: The Polemics of the Dreyfus Affair and its Aftermath* (1991). He has contributed to many volumes, including *Conservative Essays* (1978), edited by Maurice Cowling.

DR OWEN HARRIES is the editor of *The National Interest*. He taught at Sydney for many years, became personal adviser to Prime Minister Malcolm Fraser in the late 1970s, and was Australia's ambassador to UNESCO in 1982–3. He has written for many publications ranging from *Commentary* to the *New York Times*.

IRVING KRISTOL was co-founder and editor of *Encounter* between 1953 and 1960. His career has included both academic appointments and publishing, as executive vice president of Basic Books Inc. from 1969 to 1988. He has been a Fellow of the American Academy of

Arts and Sciences, and a member of the Council on Foreign Relations. He has co-edited books with Daniel Bell and Nathan Glazer, and his own most recent book is *Reflections of a Neoconservative* (1983).

DR NOEL MALCOLM was a Fellow of Gonville and Caius College, Cambridge from 1981 to 1988, and then became Foreign Editor of the *Spectator* and political columnist of the *Daily Telegraph*. He is the General Editor of the Clarendon Edition of the works of Thomas Hobbes. He has edited the complete correspondence of Thomas Hobbes in two volumes, and written a history of Bosnia. He is a Director of the Centre for Policy Studies.

PROFESSOR KENNETH MINOGUE was Professor of Political Science at the London School of Economics, and is now a Senior Research Fellow with the Social Affairs Unit. He has written for both academic and political journals, and was Chairman of the Bruges Group 1991–3. In 1986 he presented a six-part television series on free market economics. He is a director of the Centre for Policy Studies and his most recent publication is *Politics: A Very Short Introduction*.

JOHN O'SULLIVAN CBE is the Editor of the *National Review*. He was a parliamentary sketch writer for the *Daily Telegraph*, Associate Editor of the *Times* of London and the Editor of *Policy Review*. He has been a special adviser to the British Prime Minister and is on the Executive Advisory Board of the Margaret Thatcher Foundation.

DAVID PRYCE-JONES has held academic posts in America and been a special feature writer for the *Daily Telegraph* on the Middle East, China, the Soviet Union, Africa and the Balkans. He has written both novels and works of politics and history. He has also written extensively on the Palestine question, published a biography of Unity Mitford and wrote in 1988 *The Closed Circle: An Interpretation of the Arabs*. His most recent work is *The Strange Death of Soviet Communism* (1995).

DAVID WILLETTS MP moved from Oxford to the Treasury, and then to the Prime Minister's Downing Street Policy Unit, advising on economic policy, and on health and social security. His book *Modern Conservatism* was published in 1992, the same year in which he was elected MP for Havant in the general election. He was appointed an Assistant Government Whip in July 1994, and Parliamentary

Secretary in the Civil Service Department in 1996. From 1986 to 1992 he was the Director of Studies at the Centre for Policy Studies.

Foreword

POSSIBLY THE MOST FAMOUS remark I ever made is also the most misunderstood: 'There's no such thing as society.' But people forget what came next: 'There's only you and me.'

In spelling out my views I wanted to remind people that you can't pass the buck to some abstraction; that we have to take responsibility ourselves; and that making things easy for people is *not* solving the problem.

This view was memorably impressed on me when I was Secretary of State for Education. A headmistress came to see me and told me that whenever a child had a problem, she wouldn't try to smother him with sympathy, instead she would give that child a duty – to lay out the books, or to clean the blackboard. In her view the child who is given a responsibility develops a sense of self-esteem through realizing that they too have something to give and will begin to flower.

It is this sense of individual responsibility, of duty, that is the essence of individuality itself. Perhaps the greatest miracle in the world is that in spite of there being six billion people on our planet, each is different, and therefore every one of us has something unique to give. Our Christian tradition recognizes this uniqueness; the Commandments were directed at each and every one of us so that we may use our God-given talents and make a difference to the world. But that tradition also generated our belief in the rights of the individual.

We in Britain *know* that freedom incurs responsibility. We understand that for freedom to flourish it requires a framework of law; a rule of law based on equity and fairness, to guide our behaviour. These were the values from which our common law evolved, later to be built upon by the freely elected representatives of the people in Parliament.

It is this concept of liberty – yoked with a rule of law and Parliamentary sovereignty – which has triumphed in the ideological struggles of our century. Those on the left believed that under their system of total central planning and control by the self-selected few, the individual did not count. The central planners decided everything and the people obeyed. But in spite of the promises and the propaganda, their system gave neither dignity nor prosperity. It failed completely. But as Pope John Paul II declared in his encyclical *Centesimus annus*, we should not see the collapse of communism 'simply as a technical problem, but rather as a consequence of the violation of human rights to private initiative, to ownership of property and to freedom in the economic sector'.

Therefore capitalism's triumph is much more than just the triumph of one economic system over another; it is a vital element in the network of freedom and as such is a *moral quality*.

Increasingly we recognize that man's greatest asset is man himself and wherever capitalism is applied it liberates his talents and abilities. For we know that countries are not rich in proportion to their natural resources; if that were so then Russia would be the richest country in the world. She has everything: oil, gas, diamonds, platinum, gold, silver, the industrial metals, timber and a rich soil. Countries are rich whose governments have policies which encourage the essential creativity of man.

Even though we have won the great ideological battle of the century against communism, the struggle against its first cousin, socialism, has not come to an end. The two great wars of this century whetted government's appetite for increased spending. Politicians became used to wielding tremendous power and ordinary people to accepting it. In wartime it is natural that individual aspirations should take second place to a unified effort for the survival of liberty. But at the end of those wars the State was reluctant to return to the people many of the powers and responsibilities it had acquired, whether in the fields of economic management or social provision.

In peacetime, socialism kept alive the false idea that when a problem arose, the State was responsible for the solution. Arguments are always being advanced for State intervention and controls, and there are any number of vested interests – from cosy cartels to corrupt bureaucrats – anxious to advance them. But as the power of the State increases so the liberty of the citizen decreases.

The temptation remains for politicians to promise yet more in spending rather than having the courage to say 'no' to the many requests which are made. In doing so taxation replaces incentive, dependency replaces responsibility; more people look to the government for their standard of living than to their own efforts. But it remains a good rule of thumb that those countries in which the State takes a smaller share of the natural income forge ahead – and those in which the State's share swells towards or even beyond a half of GDP soon get into trouble.

We only have to look at the two most successful economies of our time – America and Japan – to see this is true. In both, government spending totals around 34 per cent or 35 per cent of GDP. In Britain the figure is about 42 per cent. But in Germany it is 49 per cent, in France 54 per cent, in Italy 53 per cent, in Denmark 63 per cent, and in Sweden a stifling 68 per cent.

The attitude of always looking to the State for solutions is the end of civilized society as we know it, for as Gibbon reflected on the fall of Athens, when the only freedom that the Athenians wanted was freedom from responsibility itself, then Athens ceased to be free.

This is why continuing the battle of ideas is so important. Politics and government are not just a matter of examining dry statistics in order to solve current problems. There must be a sense of vision and of purpose. We must lead circumstance, not be led by it.

Every generation requires a fundamental understanding of human nature, of people's desires and aspirations. Only by appreciating these can we protect our heritage of law and liberty, and promote the virtues of enterprise, responsibility and duty. The task of the politician is to apply these enduring principles to changing circumstances.

Margaret Thatcher

INTRODUCTION

ON CONSERVATIVE REALISM

KENNETH MINOGUE

'Conservative Realism' is an ambitious title. It sounds like a political takeover bid for one of the grand traditions of philosophy. In fact, nothing so ambitious is intended in these essays. What is certainly intended, however, is to point the contrast between political realities on the one hand and the aspirations which often conceal them on the other. Modern politics is dominated by big ideas about what governments should do, and conservatives take a sceptical and realist view of what big ideas can achieve. Ever since the crash of communism, Nazism and other twentieth-century projects of human transformation, some lip service at least to conservative realism has become an indispensable indication of political sanity, and its effects can be seen all around us: among President Clinton's Democrats, Tony Blair's New Labour, the Labour Parties of the Antipodes and recent election results in Canada. Yet there can be no doubt that the restless urge to social transformation still has us tossing and turning in our politics. Current productivity in the regulation industry, projects for constitutional reform, expert commissions bending their minds to solving our ills, rising public relations budgets in government (called 'educating the public'), reveal that engineering society is the one pastime people in power cannot resist. They may have given up the idea of storming Utopia; many still think they can sneak into it.

What the conservative realist knows is that utopianism feeds on itself. In politics, every solution generates new problems, and sometimes you get two for the price of one. The Prohibition Amendment in the United States greatly stimulated hoodlums to sell protection, with the result that America in the 1920s moved smoothly from one problem – alcoholism – to two problems – alcoholism *and* gangsters. This has been one of the unheeded parables of our century. It is the basic reason why government, along with its handmaiden bureaucracy, keeps on growing.

The Prohibition parable exhibits utopianism in its simplest form: first recognize an evil, and then legislate it out of existence. The process can be seen daily in journalists and politicians pointing to evils we must face, and an indignant population responding by demanding action. Indeed, the word 'active' has been found no longer active enough, and what committees now aim to be is something called 'proactive', thus corrupting politics and language at a stroke. Salvationist excitements in politics and the media are alone quite enough to keep governments busy beyond their competence, but institutional change is leading us deeper into the same morass. Europeans have now invented a whole new, and active, tier of government in Brussels, while in Britain eager nationalists want to set up parliaments of their own. With all these bodies working to eliminate evils, guarantee our safety and supervise our health, we shall soon be living in a perfect world.

In spite of a century of bitter experience, the basic assumption of modern politics is still that salvation comes from the top. Conservative realists, by contrast, think that there isn't much salvation around (certainly not in politics), and that most of it will come from the vitality and resourcefulness of the people themselves. There must, of course, be a framework of rules enforced by government, but the point of rules is not to fit people into an official blueprint, but to guide intelligent and resourceful people in pursuing their own projects so that they will not collide with each other. This kind of vitality in the people is threatened by the governmental propensity to nationalize initiative. Governments determine what industries are to be encouraged, which arts subsidized, how tourism should be planned,* what diet people should follow, how much alcohol they ought to drink, and so on. Where anything moves in society, a politician will pop up to codify it, regulate it, impose quality standards upon it, plan it, warn against it, or fit it into a national strategy. Popular resourcefulness is threatened by what one might call a vicious circle of dependency. Governments love the poor, the foolish, the clumsy, the

* The Australian Minister for Tourism in 1995 unveiled a 'national strategy' for backpackers.

gullible, the immature, the criminal, the careless, in fact inadequates of all kinds, not because of compassion or justice so much as because these are the classes of person that provide a non-stop justification for the intrusions of the civil power. Such protection is so attractive that feminists and some ethnic minorities have actually volunteered to be enlisted in the roll call of victimhood and inadequacy.

Contrariwise, governments rather dislike people who confidently make their own decisions about what to eat and drink, and how to dispose of their own resources as they themselves choose. To be independent of government advice is selfish. It lacks community spirit. Still, at least these are the people who can be taxed to the hilt so that governments can be altruistic on their behalf.

The other side of this coin is that, in their appalling busy-ness, governments fail to do what they ought to do. They should, Michael Oakeshott once wrote, under no circumstances debauch the currency, because inflation, he interestingly suggested, 'was designed to ensure our docility'.* The British Treasury certainly has no very shining record in preventing inflation. This is why Ray Evans, in this collection, focuses upon the honesty of money as a central theme of conservatism, and ends with a rousing alternative to joining the European Monetary Union, an alternative which could combine honest money with restoring sterling to its earlier international glory.

The siren call that lures governments into doing what they cannot properly do wells up from the abstract idea. The world we live in is viewed through the simplifying spectacles of social justice perhaps, or equality, or national prosperity, or democracy, and found to be seriously wanting. What that's real could possibly live up to an abstraction? Certainly no historic community such as any of the nation states of the world. In Britain and America we do in fact find justice, even plenty of social justice if we measure such a thing in welfare budgets. Equality, far from being a remote ideal, is actually something we in the West invented, and there is plenty of it in our law and mores. The same may be said of democracy, however defined, and as for prosperity, we have more of it than most human beings on the planet have ever experienced. As has often been observed,

* Michael Oakeshott, 'Conservatism: foundations and fallacies', *Daily Telegraph*, 29 June 1978.

radicals get more excited at the motes in our own eyes than at the beams in the eyes of others. The reason is, of course, that such motes supply the rhetorical leverage for more bouts of social engineering. While the framework of law must always need repair, we should remember that imperfection in society is the red badge of our freedom. No *free* society could possibly be without blemish.

Abstraction is thus the logical engine which guarantees the Pascalian restlessness of modern politics. Such trivial restlessness is fed by journalists hanging on to the tail of a scandal, or political theorists grinding their concepts into a finer and finer powder. And it has a further remarkable consequence in distorting political perspectives: the moment abstraction enters the mind of politicians, the blood and substance of the people they govern is sucked out, and they decline into ideological poster-people. The main business of such eviscerated subjects is to fit into the plans of their rulers. The conservative realist knows that actual people don't fit, and must be topped and tailed for suitability. There are many managerial devices for achieving this, of which the runaway growth of governmental agencies for public relations (what is whimsically known as 'public education') is merely the most obvious. Children in schools have during the last generation become the helpless victims of this attitudinal engineering. It has left education as little space in schools as disciplinary scholarship has had in teacher training colleges. But the same process can be seen in the vast increase in criminalizing everything from killing a bat to burying a pet in the backyard or serving beer from pint pots.

These few remarks will illustrate the fact that it is hard to be a conservative realist these days without falling into the mode of Jeremiah. Perhaps it always was. On the other hand, conservatives are likely to be rather more cheerful Jeremiahs in the 1990s because of the exhilaration they experienced during the Reagan–Thatcher years, when at least the rhetoric of government accorded with their disposition towards freedom and their hatred of the servility promoted by intellectuals who want to make society fit some pattern of perfection. Such realists will recognize, as Shirley Letwin argues in the last essay in the book, that conservatives no longer enjoy the benefits of having unambiguous dragons to slay. The time of clarion calls and clear objectives has passed, at least for the moment, but conservatives can still recognize what is free and what is unfree in the way we live now.

It is remarkable that, as Irving Kristol tells us, a third of Americans now identify themselves as conservatives – up from about zero a generation ago. And the explanation for this change will be found in his emphasis on the importance of religion in the American view of the world. Kristol's essay is notable among other things for its neo-conservative argument that in intellectual terms, communism was always too absurd to bother about, and that the real enemy was a secularizing liberalism with which conservatives had often in the past allied themselves. This suggests one possible line of thought that might respond to the problem of what conservatives can actually conserve in a world that has been serially ravaged by one big idea after another.

The antidote to the shrinkage of human substance resulting from the prevalence of abstract ideas might well be found in John O'Sullivan's account of the Humean theory of the self which has, he suggests, 'broken out of the lab' and now stalks the land as postmodernism and the politics of identity. His account of the Nixon presidency's creation by a stroke of the pen of a complete new cultural identity illustrates how an abstract idea, in this case multiculturalism, can convulse a nation.

Noel Malcolm's account of the ideas of Christian Democracy is an exercise in bringing a corpse to life. To an outsider, Christian Democracy often looks like a string of pious affirmations about the duty of the rich and powerful to sustain communal harmony by just treatment of the poor. What Malcolm shows is that this 'anti-political politics', drifting between left and right, and basically hostile to both the market and the nation state, has come into its own in post-1945 Europe and that its apparent affinity with many conservative slogans and a shared enmity to communism have misled British politicians about the nature and scope of European integration.

Richard Griffith is the contributor most concerned with the theme of abstract ideas, and in invoking Maurice Cowling and the volume of *Conservative Essays* Cowling edited in 1978 (to which both Griffith and I contributed), reminds us that what I have been calling 'conservative realism' ought not to be confused with Tory realism, a much more specific and locally rooted view of politics – one which might be described as 'poetic' rather than philosophical. Indeed, it is so specific a plant that Oakeshott, Kedourie and Letwin themselves could hardly claim it – Oakeshott because he was a philosopher, and Tory conservatism is above all not a philosophy, and Letwin and Kedourie because, like many of the present contributors, they came from abroad. Griffith lays about him with a fine hand and discovers ideology even among Eurosceptics who might be thought the last defenders of the British tradition.

David Willetts is the one contributor who might, since he is a Minister in the Major government, be able to influence events directly. His view is that 'since 1979 our Conservative governments have moved forward like ice-breakers, ploughing their way through the frozen wastes of state control'. He leaves for dead the notion that a belief in freedom, which involves leaving markets alone to get on with their business of supplying people's wants, entails a hostility to community. In particular, he fingers as a notable fallacy of recent radical thought the idea that institutions and the community are opposites. And he notes that the Victorians were very successful in moralizing the poor with virtually no help from the State at all.

In Timothy Fuller's account of a previously unpublished manuscript by Michael Oakeshott (to appear in 1996), we find a useful formulation of the basic mistake of radicalism: that it takes the world we actually live in to be merely a temporary reality to be set right. He defends conservatives against the tedious misunderstanding that their concern for the past is merely a regretful yearning to turn the clock back. Rather, conservatives use the past (as they use ideas) to help them catch sight of what is valuable in the confusing interstices of the present.

In David Pryce-Jones, we become participants in an urgent process in which layers of accumulated Western misunderstanding of the Soviet Union and the Third World are scraped away to reveal the consequences of the spread among non-Europeans of unsettling Western abstractions. His argument is all the more alarming because his diagnosis of the current direction of Europe suggests that we are following in *their* track rather than that they are following in ours. Like Owen Harries, though for almost opposite reasons, he fears that the mistakes of the past will be repeated.

Owen Harries can deal with realism in politics as a vital tradition within the discipline he knows best, namely international relations. He exhibits the kind of scepticism which allows us to treat a term such as 'realism' as a Wittgensteinian ladder. *Any* formulation of political prudence will soon find itself subverted by special interests bending its meaning to suit their purposes; hence even invoking reality is no reliable specific against illusion. All social scientists must deal with the dialectic of similarity and difference. There is a sense in which there is nothing new under the sun, and another sense in which we never step into the same river twice – or even once as the extreme sceptics would put it. Harries takes realism in international relations as a view which has many strengths, but in some versions has misled statesmen in the past, and may perhaps mislead them even more in the changed circumstances of the emerging century.

Not long before she died, Shirley Letwin gave a talk to a group of Conservative Members of Parliament at the Centre for Policy Studies, and I have added the text to these essays, partly because it illustrates the vitality and precision of her thought, and partly because it addresses, perhaps more closely even than the essays, the central question for any conservative politics: What is actually happening, and where do we seem to be going?

I

AMERICA'S 'EXCEPTIONAL CONSERVATISM'

IRVING KRISTOL

I remember the day very well, back in 1956, when I arrived at my office at *Encounter* – of which I was then co-editor – and found on my desk an unsolicited manuscript by Michael Oakeshott which he was submitting for publication. This, I thought, is the way every editor's day should begin, with an over-the-transom arrival of an essay by one of the finest living political thinkers and certainly the finest stylist. The manuscript was called 'On Being Conservative' and I read it with pleasure and appreciation. It was beautifully written, subtle in its argument, delicate in its perceptions, and full of sentences and paragraphs that merit the attention of anthologists for decades, perhaps even centuries, to come. Fortunately, this essay is to be found in his book, *Rationalism in Politics*. I say 'fortunately' because, after loving every line of this essay, I sat down and wrote to Michael, as I was then privileged to call him, rejecting it.

I forget what disingenuous circumlocutions I invented for that letter – probably something about its being both too 'abstract' and too specifically British in its frame of reference for our journal. But the truth is that, while I admired the essay immensely, I didn't really like it. Which is but another way of saying that I disagreed with it. At that time, I wasn't sure why I disagreed with it. Today, looking back over the past forty years, I can see why. I was American, Michael was English. And I was then in the earliest stages of intellectual pregnancy with those attitudes and dispositions that later emerged as 'neo-conservatism'. And American neo-conservatism is very different from the kind of ideal English conservatism that Oakeshott was celebrating so brilliantly. It is also different from the much less ideal conservatism that still dominates the Conservative Party today.

Indeed, I think it fair to say that it is different from whatever passes for conservatism in all the democracies of Western Europe today. Which doesn't necessarily mean that it is irrelevant to the politics of these nations. It does mean, however, that conservatism in America today is on a different track from that of Britain and Western Europe – I insist on the distinction – and that it is reasonable to think that one of us may be on the better track.

Oakeshott's essay, you will recall, focuses on what he calls 'the conservative disposition'. Let him describe that disposition in his own lovely language:

> To be conservative is to be disposed to think and behave in certain manners; it is to prefer certain kinds of conduct and certain conditions of human circumstances to others . . . The general characteristics of this disposition . . . centre upon a propensity to use and enjoy what is available rather than what was or what may be . . . What is esteemed is the present; and it is esteemed not on account of its connections with a remote antiquity, nor because it is recognized to be more admirable than any possible alternative, but on account of its familiarity . . . To be conservative, then, is to prefer the familiar to the unknown, to prefer the tried to the untried, fact to mystery, the actual to the possible, the limited to the unbounded, the near to the distant . . . the convenient to the perfect, present laughter to utopian bliss.

These eloquent words are bound to strike a chord in the souls of any reader, since all of us, in varying degrees, participate in such a disposition. What we call civilization is itself based on the power of this disposition. But even as I respond to Oakeshott's ideal conservatism, I know – as I knew back in 1956 – that it is not for me. And this for two reasons: First, it is irredeemably secular, as I, being a Jewish conservative, am not. Were I a Christian conservative, my reaction would be the same. For it is impossible for any religious person to have the kinds of attitudes toward the past and the future that Oakeshott's conservative disposition celebrates. Our Scriptures and our daily prayer book link us to the past and to the future with an intensity lacking in Oakeshott's vision. Not that this religious dimension of our humanity in any way necessarily denigrates the present, in all its fullness. Judaism especially, being a more this-worldly religion than Christianity, moves us to sanctify the present in our daily lives – but always reminding us that we are capable of doing so only through God's grace to our distant forefathers. Similarly, it is incumbent upon us to link our children and grandchildren to this 'great chain of being', however suitable or unsuitable *their* present might be to our conservative disposition. And, of course, the whole purpose of sanctifying the present is to prepare humanity for a redemptive future.

In short, Oakeshott's ideal conservative society is a society without religion, since all religions bind us as securely to past and future as to the present. The conservative disposition is real enough, but without the religious dimension, it is thin gruel. The conservative disposition can have no singular, unmediated existence because it is never the only disposition in anyone's character. In addition to the conservative disposition, there is what might be called the 'theotropic' disposition. Just as, in all societies known to us, Oakeshott's conservative disposition is plainly visible, so is the religious disposition. In the concluding sentence of his inaugural lecture at the London School of Economics, Oakeshott made that magnificent declaration to the effect that this is the best of all possible worlds and everything in it is a necessary evil. That is more a biblical assertion than a philosophical one. In any case, his conservative disposition offers us no guidance in coping with all those necessary evils, which can tear our lives apart and destroy whatever philosophical equanimity we have achieved as a result of reading the writers of philosophy.

Secondly, Oakeshott's conservative disposition runs squarely against the American grain. Oh, Americans possess such a disposition all right. Despite all one reads about the frustrations of American life, it is the rare American who dreams of moving to another land, and hardly any do. We are, in some respects, a very conservative people – but not quite in the Oakeshottian sense.

To begin with, we have a most emphatic and explicit relation to our past – an 'ideological' relation, some would say. In the United States today, all school children, in all fifty states, begin their day with a recitation of the Pledge of Allegiance to the flag and to the Constitution of the United States of America. There is no national legislation to this effect; it is entirely up to the states. Despite some efforts by radical educators, no state has removed this prescription.

In addition, there is the extraordinary fact that at the opening of every high school, college, and professional sporting event – and high school and college sports are major foci of attention for Americans – players and spectators rise to their feet and sing the national anthem. And it is not a good idea to fail to do so, if you wish to avoid hostile encounters with your fellow countrymen. It is easy to say, without fear of contradiction, that the United States today is the most vibrantly patriotic of all the Western democracies. Some might say – a sophisticated European would surely be tempted to say – that this merely demonstrates that the United States is, in some crucial respects, a pre-modern country. Perhaps so. Or perhaps we are a post-modern country; one should not blandly exclude that possibility.

Behind this ideological patriotism is the fact, noted by all historians and observers, that the United States is a 'creedal' nation. Being American has nothing to do with ethnicity, or blood-ties of any kind, or lineage, or length of residence even. What we scornfully call 'nativism' in the United States is what passes for authentic patriotism among many Germans and Frenchmen. None of this is surprising if one recalls that the United States is, literally, a nation of immigrants, and in the course of time has developed astonishing powers of assimilation. What is surprising is the intensity of partiotism generated by this fact, an intensity owing to the great fact that assimilation in the United States bears a resemblance to a conversion experience, in which a new creed replaces an old. No one ever really expected that. One might easily have expected the opposite, as many did. Ironically, that opposite reaction is now being sponsored by the left in the guise of 'multiculturalism', which has practically nothing to do with culture and everything to do with politics. So far, at any rate, the impact on American patriotism has been minimal, being limited to a fraction of the educated elite.

This 'creed' and this ideological fervour is suffused with a kind of religious sensibility. Indeed, American patriotism was born out of, and was sustained for our first two centuries by, the sensibility of Protestant dissent. In the last two centuries, our increasingly secular outlook has tempered this sensibility, so that sociologists now blandly refer to an American 'civic religion' that unites the community with secular ties. The concept of a 'civic religion' has its validity, up to a point. We are no longer the 'nation under God', a providential nation, as we once casually defined ourselves. But that reservoir of religiosity, though now diminished, is still there, and these still waters run deep. Most Americans thought Soviet communism to be an awful idea, and a terrible reality, simply because it was 'atheistic and godless', and therefore doomed. And they didn't have to read Hayek to come to this conclusion. Scholars may debate the reasons for the collapse of Soviet communism, which surprised so many of them. The ordinary American was less astonished.

There are tensions between American religiosity and the more secular 'civic religion', but they coexist because they also have much in common. They subscribe equally to a somewhat less rigorous version of the Judaeo-Christian moral tradition. Both are individualistic when it comes to economic matters, wedding the Protestant ethic (at least in Max Weber's version) to the philosophy of Adam Smith. Both approve of economic growth, as a character-building exercise and as a way of improving the human condition. And both are, in general, future-oriented and 'progressive' in their political vision. When Americans deplore the present, and even when they do so in comparison with the past, they always assume that ameliorative possibilities are available. American politics is about those ameliorative possibilities and the controversial choices they entail. And today there is so much to deplore in this present that Oakeshott's paean to present-mindedness is singularly inapt.

All of this is by way of background explanation to my own problem with Oakeshott's writings and to the fact that these writings do not have and will not have any large appeal to Americans. I can speak from bitter experience here. When I was an editor with the publishing house Basic Books, I published the American edition of *Rationalism in Politics*. It sold 600 copies.

But it is also by way of a background explanation to what I see as a major divergence between American conservatism today and British as well as European conservatism. It is a divergence with significant implications for the future of the Western democracies. The difference can be summed up this way: Conservatism in America today is a *movement*, a popular movement, not a faction within any political party. Though, inevitably, most conservatives vote Republican, they are not Party loyalists and the Party has to woo them to win their votes. This movement is issued-oriented. It will happily meld with the Republican Party if the Party is 'right' on the issues. If not, it will walk away. This troubled relationship between the conservative movement and the Republican Party is a key to the understanding of American politics today. The conservative movement has become a powerful force within the Party, but it does not dominate the Party. And there is no possibility of the Party ever dominating the movement.

Post-World War Two American conservatism begins to take shape with the American publication of Hayek's *The Road to Serfdom* in 1943 and the founding in 1955 of William F. Buckley's *National Review*. Previously, there had been a small circle who were admirers of the Jeffersonian, quasi-anarchist, teachings of the likes of Albert Jay Nock, but no one paid much attention to them. Hayek's polemic against socialism did strike a chord, however, especially among members of the business community as well as existing conservative groups. There may have been people converted from 'statism' to 'anti-statism' by that book, but my impression is that most admirers of the book were already anti-statist and pro-free market. What Hayek did was to mobilize them intellectually, and to make their views more respectable. I have to confess that I still haven't got around to reading *The Road to Serfdom*, though I am a great admirer of Hayek's later writings in intellectual history and political philosophy. The reason was, and is, that not for a moment did I believe that the United States was (or is) on any kind of road to serfdom. Socialism has never had much of a presence in America and, besides, having gone through a brief Trotskyist phase in my college days, I needed no instruction on socialist illusions or the evils of Soviet communism.

Still, it is fair to say that an anti-socialist, anti-communist, anti-statist perspective dominated the thinking and politically active part of American conservatism from the end of World War Two to the Goldwater campaign of 1964. William F. Buckley's *National Review* faithfully represented this point of view and it gradually helped recruit enough younger political activists to become a force within the Republican Party. The Goldwater débâcle revealed how limited a force it was. But it was strong enough to dominate the Republican Party, just as the McGovern débâcle of 1972 did not prevent the left from dominating the Democratic Party. The Nixon elections of 1968 and 1972, however, revealed that, even when winning elections – largely through Democratic default – the basic principles of post-war conservatism had little purchase on American realities and had to be admixed with a large portion of fumbling opportunism. And yet, from the ashes of the Goldwater–Nixon débâcles there arose Ronald Reagan, to become a popular two-term President only a few years later. What happened?

What happened, I would say, was two things. First, though certainly not in order of political significance, was the emergence of an intellectual trend that later came to be called 'neo-conservatism'. This current of thought, in which I was deeply involved, differed in one crucial respect from its conservative predecessors: its chosen enemy was contemporary liberalism, not socialism or statism in the abstract. (About communism – as distinct, say, from Soviet foreign policy – we had almost nothing to say, we were so utterly hostile to it.) The dozen or so academics and intellectuals who formed the original core of neo-conservatism, located at *The Public Interest*, a journal Daniel Bell and I founded in 1965, were all disillusioned liberals: disillusioned with the newest twists and turns of that liberalism, but also (in varying degrees) with their past liberalism whose inherent philosophical (even metaphysical) flaws now rose to visibility. We were, most of us, social scientists, but there were no economists in the group. Anti-statism, as distinguished from anti-liberalism, has, yesteryear as today, been the chosen passion of economists.

In a way, the symbol of the influence of neo-conservative thinking on the Republican Party was the fact that Ronald Reagan could praise Franklin D. Roosevelt as a great American president – praise echoed by Newt Gingrich a dozen years later – and this is no longer so surprising. The message was clear: the Republican Party was no longer interested in destroying the welfare state, in the name of 'anti-statism', but intended rather to reconstruct it along more economical and more humane lines. The emphasis on more 'humane' is another sign of neo-conservative influence. Whereas traditional conservatism had tried to focus attention on welfare cheating, the writings of various neo-conservatives over the years emphasized the terrible, demoralizing effects of our welfare system on the recipients of welfare themselves. It was no longer a matter of simply saving the budget from welfare expenditures but of redeeming the welfare population from the kind of 'exploitation' involved in a system that created and encouraged dependency. The new message – that dependency corrupts and that absolute dependency tends to corrupt absolutely – gave a moral dimension to welfare reform that it had lacked. In the United States, there can be no successful reform movement without such a moral dimension.

To the surprise of most observers, the critique of liberalism by neo-conservative intellectuals, scholars, and publicists was in some ways more effective than the older attack on 'statism'. Paradoxically, precisely because there was no socialist movement, no ideological 'statist' movement in the United States, the neo-conservative critique went deeper, and was more radical, than conservative critiques in Britain or Western Europe.

Oakeshott has evoked little active response, as distinct from passive admiration, in the United States, but the writings of Leo Strauss have been extraordinarily influential. Strauss's analysis of the destructive elements within modern liberalism, an analysis that was popularized by his students and his students' students, has altered the very tone of public discourse in the United States. Who would have thought it possible, thirty years ago, that in 1995, one third of the American public would designate itself as conservative while only 17 per cent designated itself as liberal, with the rest claiming the label of 'moderate'. To bring contemporary liberalism into disrepute – its simplistic views of human nature, its utopian social philosophy, its secularist animus against religion – is no small achievement.

The second, and most spectacular thing that happened was the emergence of religious conservatives, especially Protestant evangelical conservatives, as a force to be reckoned with. This has no parallel in any of the other Western democracies, where secularist habits of thought still rule supreme. It has been estimated that something like one third of the American electorate are (or claim to be) regular church-goers. Not all of them are conservative, of course, but the overwhelming majority are. And it is important to emphasize that, in so far as they are anti-statist, as most are, it is not only on economic grounds, or even of Jeffersonian–individualist grounds. These religious conservatives see, quite clearly and correctly, that statism in America is organically linked with secular liberalism, that many of the programmes and activities of the welfare state have a powerful anti-religious animus. School prayer is a very live issue among religious conservatives, not because public schools are especially suitable places for young people to pray in, but because our educational system, dominated by the teachers' unions, the schools of education, and the liberal politicians who count on their active electoral support, is biased in an anti-religious way. And because this religious conservatism is not only anti-statist but anti-liberal on philosophical grounds (however 'unsophisticated' these philosophical grounds are), the role of neo-conservative intellectuals has become especially important.

Conservative politicians woo the religious conversatives, but only neo-conservatives can really speak to them. The intellectual class in the United States is so violently opposed to religious conservatism that the presence of even a relatively small number of friendly neo-conservatives makes a difference. Many of these neo-conservatives are not themselves religiously observant in their private lives, though more and more are coming to be. This leads to accusations by liberal intellectuals of hypocrisy or cold-blooded political instrumentalism. But such accusations miss the point. All political philosophers prior to the twentieth century, regardless of their personal piety or lack thereof, understood the importance of religion in the life of the political community. Neo-conservatives, because of their interest in and attachment to classical (as distinct from contemporary) political philosophy, share this understanding. Just as there is a difference between being pious and being observant, so there is a difference between being observant and being religious. As it happens, a disproportionate number of neo-conservatives are Jewish, and within the Jewish community such distinctions have always been blurred. In any case, more and more Christians and Jews these days, who themselves have a secular lifestyle, are seeing to it that their children are raised within a religious tradition. Modern secularism has such affinities to moral nihilism that even those who wish simply to affirm or reaffirm moral values have little choice but to seek a grounding for such values in a religious tradition.

Most foreign journalists, like their American counterparts, tend to be secularist in outlook and therefore have difficulty in understanding what is happening within American politics. One has only to read the American reporting in such a distinguished journal as *The Economist* to experience this difficulty – to read reporting that is sophisticated, blandly superficial, and misleading. But it is not only the issue of religion that creates this difficulty. There is also the equally significant issue of populism.

American democracy regularly witnesses populist upsurges. European and British observers, along with most American scholars, tend to describe them as 'spasms', or even 'paroxysms'. But they are nothing of the sort. They are built into the very structure of American politics in a way that is alien to British or European politics, where 'politics' is what the government says or does. In a sense, it is fair to say that contemporary political journalism as well as most political scholarship is 'statist' in its preconceptions and vision. Whenever a populist upsurge occurs, as is the case today, national politics in the United States trails behind local politics, and focusing one's attention on Washington is a case of misdirection.

In the United States, most school boards are locally elected, and school board politics is the way most adult Americans begin their political education. If you are looking for some of the reasons for the strength of American conservatism today, watching local school board politics is a good, though difficult place to begin – difficult because there are so many such school boards, and the issues that cause contention vary from place to place. Still, had one been paying attention, one would be better prepared to appreciate the anxieties and frustrations of so many American parents with the educational establishment. It is not simply that their children do not often get a decent education in the basics of reading, writing, arithmetic, history, and geography, but that the 'youth culture' and 'counterculture' born after World War Two has captured the school system itself, and has been codified in the leading schools of education. Parents are loath to argue with educators, who are presumed to be the experts, and when they do argue they are sufficiently confused and intimidated to argue badly. But anxiety about what happens to their children, a diffuse terror, even, about what kinds of mature young people they will grow up to be, is widespread in the United States today. Sooner or later, politicians emerge to tap this kind of anxiety. That is why the so-called 'social issues', more accurately described as moral issues, are so powerful today. The Clinton Administration, convinced (as most liberals are) that economic issues are at the centre of politics, finds itself bewildered and impotent when confronted by such issues. Economic frustration liberals are sensitive to, but moral frustration is incomprehensible to them. The major reason for this incomprehension, of course, is that it is the doctrines of modern liberalism itself that have given rise to this frustration.

In Washington, DC, the most liberal and 'statist' city in the nation, school board politics across the country is unworthy of the attention of the national media, as is state and local politics for the most part. Indeed, our liberal media really detest our entire federal system, which complicates their journalistic mission. They don't mind presidential primaries or primaries for governorships, which fit into their framework of politics-as-a-horse-race. But they hate primaries for lower offices: that's 'local news' and unworthy of their attention. Referenda – a legacy of the progressive movement that is institutionalized in many of our states – are now equally despised because they introduce a 'wild card' into the established political 'game', and because these days are more successfully used by conservative activists. They are horrified by politicians who mix religion with politics, since our secular liberal media is convinced that religion is, at best, a private affair and has no place at all in the public square. A politician who so much as mentions Jesus Christ alarms them.

Ironically, Washington and the liberal media are least prepared for conservative changes within the media itself. These changes have come from an unexpected source – from yesteryear's technology, not today's. There is a comfortable symbiosis between our national news magazines, our half-dozen or so newspapers that claim national attention, and our national TV networks. They are all liberal, more or less, and feel that they share the journalistic mission of 'enlightening' (as well as entertaining) the American public. They have tried, somewhat less than half-heartedly, to give 'representation' to the conservative viewpoint whenever they sense that this viewpoint has become popular. But they were utterly unprepared for the sudden emergence and swift rise of radio 'talk shows', which now rival TV's daytime soap operas in popularity. These talk shows are overwhelmingly conservative in their politics and populist in their rhetoric – which is another way of saying that they are, more often than not, stridently conservative, vulgarly conservative, and not at all urbane or sophisticated.

All of this happened without anyone planning it, or directing it, or even anticipating it. It was made possible by the federal structure of our polity and by the fact that there are well over a thousand local radio stations. Once a local programme – a Rush Limbaugh, for instance – becomes popular, other local stations, always eager for listeners, will rush to broadcast him. And if, for competitive reasons, they cannot do so, they will try hard to invent their own popular conservative talk shows. The owners of these stations are interested primarily in making some money, not in spreading any kind of liberal 'enlightenment'. And, given the near absence of government regulation, the market works.

In the United States, there is always a latent populist potential simply because the structure of our polity and of our economy makes it possible for *vox populi* to find expression. There are obstacles to overcome, of course, but not too many and not too large. This populist potential disturbs political theorists, even conservative ones who fear that populist dissatisfaction is likely to have an anti-capitalist thrust. In fact, this has rarely been the case in the United States. Even the original populist movement at the beginning of this century, generally identified as belonging to the left, was not really so. It was hostile to big business, not to the free market, and the big business it opposed were the 'trusts', the emerging monopolies and quasi-monopolies that then were becoming dominant economic institutions. The populist response was to 'break them up', so as to re-establish free enterprise and a competitive marketplace. The idea of nationalizing large corporations is almost never on the populist agenda, and the idea of governments regulating them rather than disassembling them was very grudgingly accepted as a second best. It is interesting to note that today populist opinion, as every poll shows, is more concerned about cutting the federal deficit than about lowering taxes, which has come as a great surprise to many conservatives, who learned in their political science courses in college that 'the people' always want to be pandered to. It is also worth noting that the current Republican Congress is turning a cold shoulder to the lobbyists of the major corporations while exuding friendliness to those organizations that represent smaller businesses. This upsets many conservative economists who point to macrostatistics that show the economic importance of multinational corporations. Which only shows that the macrostatistics of economists, along with the microstatistics of the public opinion polls, are best ignored by a conservative government that is interested not merely in being re-elected but in creating an enduring, national conservative majority. Economists are always complaining that politicians are usually too short-sighted, thereby revealing themselves to be too often politically myopic.

As concerns foreign policy, too, the new conservative populism is playing a crucial – though as yet ambiguous – role in an interesting political realignment that is occurring. The liberal Democrats, ever since the 1930s, have generally been interventionist and multilateralist in foreign policy. The conservative Republicans have tended to be nationalist and isolationist. This situation is changing. Liberal Democrats are now well on their way to being economic protectionists and are much less interested in seeing the United States play a major role in world affairs. In contrast, Republicans now favour international free trade and, while still nationalist, are no longer isolationist. Just how those trends, still embryonic, will develop in the future is unknowable. The Republicans have a special problem in defining a nationalist foreign policy in a post-Cold War world. But one thing is clear. Multilateralism is dead, so far as both parties are concerned. This is something our European allies (and our own State Department) seem not to understand. It isn't that American opinion has turned hostile to the United Nations and NATO. Rather, there isn't enough interest in such organizations to breed hostility.

The populist conservatism that is the major trend in American conservatism also has its own internal problems. There are still a lot of traditional conservatives who are suspicious of populism. Many of them are still in the Senate, which is elected for longer terms and in staggered stages. But even in the House of Representatives there is internal dissension. The 'right to life' movement, like the abolitionists of a century and a half ago, are fanatically determined to make the best the enemy of the good. Partial victories they tend to regard as a distraction from the total victory they seek. And then there are all those newly-elected Republican governors, critical of the welfare state but reluctant to give up federal funds that help them cope with their own budgetary shortfalls. In short, all talk about an abrupt 'conservative resolution' is dangerous hyperbole, even if it does inspire the troops. There will surely be defeats ahead, some of them self-inflicted.

The United States today shares all of the evils, all of the problems, to be found among the Western democracies, and sometimes in an exaggerated form. But it is also the case that the United States today is the only Western democracy that is witnessing a serious conservative revival that is an active response to these evils and problems. The further fact that it is a populist conservatism dismays the conservative elites of Britain and Western Europe, who prefer a more orderly and dignified kind of conservatism which, in actuality, always turns out to be a defensive and therefore enfeebled conservatism. It is certainly true that any kind of populism can be a danger to our democratic orders. But it is also true that populism can be a corrective to the defects of democratic order, defects often arising from the intellectual influence, and the skilful entrepreneurial politics, of our democratic elites. Classical political thought was wary of democracy because it saw the people as fickle, envious, and inherently turbulent. They had no knowledge of democracies where the people were conservative and the educated elites that governed them were ideological elites, always busy provoking disorder and discontent so as to achieve some utopian goal. Populist conservatism is a distinctly modern phenomenon, and conservative thinking has not yet caught up with it. That is why the 'exceptional' kind of conservative politics we are now witnessing in the United States is so important, and is to be looked at seriously. It could turn out to represent the 'last, best hope' of contemporary conservatism.

What would Michael Oakeshott have made of this populist conservatism? I don't for a moment think he would have admired it. But Michael was a very wise man, and I believe he might very well consider it as one of those 'necessary evils' in this 'best of all possible worlds'. I would like to think so, anyhow.

II

CONSERVATISM AND CULTURAL IDENTITY

JOHN O'SULLIVAN

In his review of Andrew Motion's biography of Philip Larkin, Martin Amis gave a strong and, given that he was writing for the *New Yorker*, brave defence of Larkin against the charges of sexism, racism, moral squalor, etc then making the literary rounds. Much of this defence was built around the idea that Larkin had grown up and lived at a time when racism, as now defined, was so common as not to deserve censure, and when sexism did not exist as a category of sin into which one could fall. Evidently feeling, however, that he needed to guard Larkin against the secondary charge of making no effort at all to move when the times did, indeed of resisting any such movement with determination, Amis embarked on the following philosophical exercise:

> Larkin the man is separated from us, historically, by changes in the self. For his generation, you were what you were, and that was that. It made you unswervable and adamantine. My father has this quality. I don't. None of us do. There are too many forces at work on us. There are too many fronts to cover. In the age of self-improvement, the self is inexorably self-conscious . . . [Larkin] couldn't change the cards he was dealt.

Amis here is making an important point and two minor mistakes. The first minor mistake is of thinking of his father, Kingsley Amis, as some kind of typical spokesman for his generation. That must be one of the stranger effects bred by familiarity.

The second mistake is the familiar one of generational parochialism in a broader sense. We all have the illusion that the world in which we grew up was a much more fixed and stable affair than the one in which we make our adult way. And, in particular, because life itself is a training in psychological sophistication, we naturally see ourselves and our friends as more complex, variable and *interesting* than the simple manly men and womanly women whom we met around our parents' dinner table. This illusion led Amis to get his dates wrong. The concept of the self, or of personal identity, as something changeable, uncertain, and shaped and continually reshaped by external pressures goes back at least to Hume and, as we shall see, has been a staple of modern literature and psychology for about a century.

Amis's important insight, however, was that this concept of the identity has developed so radically – the self being now seen as almost infinitely malleable – and has been so widely popularized, moving from the philosophy lecture room to the cinema, that it is now challenging a much older religious and social concept of identity, built around such ideas as conscience and the soul. As in a 1950s science fiction movie, this modern theory of identity has broken out of the laboratory and is stalking through the town, inserting itself into the heads of regular citizens, and transforming them into other-directed aliens. And since how we think of ourselves determines so much, from the upbringing of children to the treatment of criminals, the conflict between these two theories is one of literally human proportions.

Of course, both theories start out with a great deal in common. They agree, in fact, that the self is put together from constituent qualities bequeathed by the usual suspects, Nature and Nurture. Where they disagree is, first, in judging what holds these constituent parts together in an individual identity (if anything does), and secondly, in determining whether the resulting identity is authentically individual or a bogus one imposed from without.

Let me begin, then, by outlining the points of rough agreement: an individual identity is put together from three elements, or sets of elements. The first is that set of psychological abilities which seem to be innate to all human beings and which become evident in the early years of childhood. These are consciousness, memory, and the moral sense.

Consciousness makes us aware of our existence separate from others. Memory extends that awareness backward through time. And the moral sense tells us the terms on which we should deal with those others. Consciousness, memory and the moral sense together generate that part of identity that we call the conscience. This is more than just a voice telling us not to take wrong actions in the here and now. It forces us to feel moral responsibility for past actions, and so helps to establish identity as something that exists through time.

Let me illustrate the point. It is sometimes said of a vicious criminal who has undergone a moral transformation in prison and performed great charitable or scholarly works, that he should be released because he is clearly 'no longer the man who committed the crimes'. But would the criminal himself agree with this? Ian Brady, the Moors murderer, who became a Christian in prison (but who has performed no great works), is on record as saying that someone who has committed such crimes as his has indefinitely forfeited any right of release. Another such criminal might, of course, wish to be released, but almost certainly on the grounds that he had purged his offences. If so, that would be an admission of a continuing moral responsibility and so, in effect, a claim of identity extending through time. Indeed, the great likelihood is that criminals like the 'Birdman of Alcatraz', who seemed to experience a moral transformation, performed their good works precisely because they felt they *were* the same men who had committed the monstrous crimes and they wanted to build up an equally impressive list of services on the opposite side of the moral ledger. They wanted to atone.

The conscience is, of course, common to all human beings except psychopaths and editors. Its component parts – memory, consciousness and the moral sense – are, however, only the first building block of identity. They make us aware of our individuality, but they do not alone constitute it. The second set of qualities making up identity is our genetic inheritance from our particular parents. It is this inheritance that sets us on the road to being individuals by laying down our potential abilities, tastes and temperaments. Psychologists seem to have established that this inheritance is extraordinarily rich and influential. We are, it seems, predisposed by our individual genes to have a particular level of IQ, to enter particular occupations, to attend particular churches, to marry a particular kind of spouse, to be law-abiding or criminal, mad or sane, healthy or sick, friendly or suspicious, shy or forward, party animal or wall-flower, long- or short-lived, and even, as W. S. Gilbert foretold, 'either a little Liberal, or else a little Conservative'.

And as a child grows older, both he and other people come to recognize that he has a particular cocktail of personality traits. Every school class has a class hero, a class clown, a class swot (or nerd), a class bully, a class victim, and a class athlete. These identities cling. His fellows come to expect certain kinds of behaviour from him; he learns to provide or modify them as popularity dictates.

Which brings us to the third element in identity: the influence of environment. In Ira Levin's thriller, *The Boys from Brazil*, Dr Josef Mengele contrives the birth of several clones of Hitler, genetically identical to the Führer, quite literally 'little Hitlers'. But even a dedicated Nazi recognizes that genetics is not enough. A genetic clone of Hitler, brought up in different circumstances, might become almost anything and anyone: possibly another terrorist leader, improbably a charismatic benefactor of mankind, most likely a mediocre architect. So he arranges for the adoption of his charges by families who fit the description of Hitler's parents: a middle-aged civil servant married to a younger woman. And he completes the environmental conditioning by having the husbands murdered at the same age as Hitler's father had died.

We are left in suspense at the end of the novel as to how Mengele's plot will turn out; but it seemed to me to contain one obvious flaw. These infant Hitlers were deposited in several countries: capitalist America, social democratic Sweden, and pre-Thatcher Britain, as well as modern Germany. There must at least be the possibility, perverse from Mengele's standpoint, of Germany's being conquered and forced to adopt a regime of politically correct social democracy by a ruthless Swedish dictator suffering from an especially neurotic case of cognitive dissonance.

For many of the most important components of identity arise from our being born in a particular family, in a particular place, at a particular time in history, and therefore into a particular set of traditions and customs. To take the most intimate example, the first language we learn is an accident of birth. Our religious identity is something we embrace long before we can grasp its importance or implications. Our sexuality is probably determined in the main genetically, but how we regard it is at least strongly influenced by social custom. We pick up the manners of our social class, assuming them to be universal laws of good behaviour. We have a natural tendency to emulate our parents, whether they are loving, decent, dutiful people, or selfish, neglectful and drunken layabouts. We obtain automatic and apparently indefeasible membership in our nation or ethnic group, together with a legacy of accompanying songs, myths, and stories. And all of these things, though external and pre-existing, are absorbed by our fledgling identity and become as much a part of us as our temperament, our IQs or our digestion.

Indeed, perhaps more so. When asked to account for ourselves, we give our family name, our sex, our nationality, our religious affiliation, our social class, even in recent years our sexual preference. We rarely volunteer our IQ or tell the Census officer that we are introverts – nor even that we are extroverts. Some of the most important elements of our identity are external, accidental and above all social.

From the point of view of the traditional theory of identity – what I shall henceforth call the conservative theory – that poses little or no problem. 'Art is man's nature,' said Burke, and man is a social animal who draws upon social materials in building his identity. Does this constitute an unnatural imposition by society upon the individual identity? Not at all. Without the influence of society, a person's identity would be like Hobbes's description of natural society: solitary, poor, nasty, brutish and short (and, one might add, speechless). The social elements in identity are the means whereby someone's natural gifts and dispositions are made manifest to the rest of the world.

And as we grow older, we also grow increasingly discriminating in the use we make of the social elements of our identity. We reflect upon our condition and circumstances, which is why, incidentally, we cannot be successfully conditioned. We may quietly reject some of the things our parents hold dear. We may change our religion. Or take a more detached view of our country, even changing our citizenship. Or learn a new set of manners, whether as conscious social climbing or simply through frequent exposure to a different class. As William Letwin wrote in *Policy Review*, reviewing a book by one Professor Green: '. . . "the environment" is not an objective fact which can be assessed accurately by an objective observer. Instead, each individual largely shapes his own environment by emphasizing some of its aspects while ignoring others, by interpreting its manifestations according to his own beliefs, and by directly acting upon it. Professor Green . . . errs in regarding "the environment" as something that forms each person rather than as something largely and differently formed by each person.' Or, as Shirley Letwin wrote in *The Anatomy of Thatcherism*: 'A human being in possession of his faculties is never merely potter's clay. He is himself both potter and clay because he necessarily decides what to make of whatever happens to him.'

What, however, is the 'person' who does this shaping and choosing? What is the entity that draws upon the different materials in 'the environment' and combines them with consciousness, memory, moral sense, and genetic endowment to shape – and perhaps, as time goes by, to reshape – a particular individual identity?

The religious answer to this question is the soul, a soul which is implicated in both the psychological dispositions of identity and the physical movements of the body. My argument here is not that the soul controls identity in a manipulative way, as a driver controls a train, but that it is at the core of identity and that consciousness, memory, genetic endowment, language, nationality and all the rest form, so to speak, concentric trenches around it, inhabited by simultaneous translators, theologians, lawyers, strategists, games-players and, above all, public relations advisers through whom it deals with external reality.

For practical purposes, it makes little difference whether one calls this entity a soul or gives it some secular explanation such as the Freudian trio of id, ego and superego. What matters is that both describe a central core of identity.

Of course, one cannot demonstrate such a thing, and I am aware that this account contradicts the current wisdom of philosophy and psychology. But it is also in accord with a psychological conviction which most people, including even sceptical philosophers, seem to hold intuitively. So, one must ask sceptics some questions: Suppose the soul to be an illusion; is it not an extremely solid one? If the psychological reality of identity includes consciousness, memory, moral reasoning, practical and prudential calculation, a feeling of free will and of moral responsibility for the actions of the person (including even those actions which cannot be wholly remembered as, for instance, actions performed when drunk), how does the real thing differ from the illusion of a soul? And, furthermore, if abandoning the illusion leads to dangerous practical consequences, as I shall argue, should we not pause to consider those consequences before we throw out the psyche with the psychobabble?

For it is this concept of a natural core of identity that the modern theories of identity reject, and there is a variety of identities nominated to replace the traditional one. They all, however, begin by attempting to discredit the notion of a central core of identity as possessing a reality separate from its experiences. Thus, David Hume writes:

> For my part, when I enter most intimately into what I call *myself*, I always stumble on some particular perception or other, of heat or cold, light or shade, love or hatred, pain or pleasure. I never catch *myself* at any time without a perception, and never can observe anything but the perception. When my perceptions are removed for any time, as by sound sleep; so long am I insensible of *myself*, and may truly be said not to exist . . . I may venture to affirm of the rest of mankind, that they are nothing but a bundle or collection of different perceptions, which succeed each other with an inconceivable rapidity and are in a perpetual flux and movement. Our eyes cannot turn in their sockets without varying our perceptions . . . The mind is a kind of theatre, where several perceptions successively make their appearance; pass, re-pass, glide away, and mingle in an infinite variety of postures and situations. There is properly no *simplicity* in it at one time, nor *identity* in different; whatever natural propension we may have to imagine that simplicity and identity.*

If there is no there there, however, how can we account for the illusion of one? Quite simply, that it is a false identity put there by other people: your parents, your neighbours, your countrymen and, if you are a child of seven or under, the Jesuits. This false identity consists not only of the digested influences of class, nation, locality,

* David Hume, *A Treatise of Human Nature*, ed. L. A. Selby-Bigge, 2nd Edn revised by P. H. Niddich, Oxford: Clarendon Press, 1980, Book I, Part IV, c. 6, pp. 252–3.

sex and so on, but also of the moral consciousness we feel to exist at the centre of our being. So even if there is some kind of instinctual moral sense, as James Q. Wilson argues, the moral rules through which it expresses itself have been put there by other people – respectable society, your parents, the church. For one school of theorists, notably Marx, liberation consists precisely of freeing yourself from this kind of false consciousness.

According to the more radical philosophers, however, the man who liberates himself from this primitive prison of false identity does not thereby achieve autonomy. No such luck. He stumbles out on to a crowded stage, and he is there handed a variety of masks which he assumes in response to the hints, shouts, murmurs, and prompts from other actors in a play jointly co-authored by Hume and Pirandello. Here is Laudisi, a character in Pirandello's *It Is So If You Think So*, explaining the theory to Signora Sirelli:

> *Laudisi*: Now, you have touched me, have you not? And you see me? And you are absolutely sure about me, are you not? Well now, madam, I beg of you; do not tell your husband, nor my sister, nor my niece, nor Signora Cini here, what you think of me; because, if you were to do that, they would all tell you that you are completely wrong. But, you see, you are completely right: because I am really what you take me to be; though, my dear madam, that does not prevent me also being really what your husband, my sister, my niece, and Signora Cini take me to be – because they too are absolutely right!
>
> *Signora Sirelli*: In other words you are a different person for each of us.
>
> *Laudisi*: Of course I'm a different person! And you, madam, pretty as you are, aren't you a different person, too?
>
> *Signora Sirelli* [hastily]: No siree! I assure you, as far as I'm concerned, I'm always the same always, yesterday, today, and forever!
>
> *Laudisi*: Ah, but so am I, from my point of view, believe me! And, I would say that you are all mistaken unless you see me as I see myself; but that would be an inexcusable presumption on my part – as it would on yours, my dear madam!

Here is a world in which identities are created by situations. What holds a personality together really is a set of skills for coping with external reality. Identities are mere roles or masks we use to deal with other people. In which case, of course, our identities are in effect created by others in a much more radical sense than in Freud or Marx. In the primitive notions of false consciousness, the villains plant their ideas in our heads and then depart, leaving us with our personal neuroses and reactionary social ideas. But in the more radical versions, other people are constantly rewiring the insides of our heads.

These ideas have spread widely in philosophy, sociology, psychology and dinner-table conversation, so that people as different as psychologist Robert J. Lifton, with his notion of the Protean self, or David Riesman, with his idea of the 'other-directed man', may be thought to be expressing variations on them. It is, however, Woody Allen who has produced the *reductio ad absurdum* of this theory in his film *Zelig*, the story of a man so responsive to the expectations of others and the influences of social environment that he becomes in succession a radical communist, a Hooverite conservative, an orthodox Jew, and a Nazi. And, of course, he is able to assume these various identities convincingly because he is conscious of an inner emptiness – the lack of an authentic identity of his own.

Here then is the existential choice offered to us by the modern theories of identity: we can be either the puppets of other people, dummies surrounded by ventriloquists, or the landlords of a vacant lot.

This is, of course, an intolerable choice. But it offers one attractive escape hatch: if other people can insert a false identity into the empty space in my head, can I perhaps insert an authentic self there in its place? Authentic because rationally chosen and consciously shaped by myself rather than simply a psychological 'given' I gradually discover in childhood and adolescence. And the principle upon which this new identity can be selected is the best bonus of all. That principle has been laid down by the greatest living American psychologist, Tom Wolfe, in his essay 'The Me Decade'. It began life as an advertising slogan for a shampoo: 'If I have only life to live, let me live it as a blonde.'

The charm of this principle for constructing a new identity is that it is almost infinitely accommodating. It enables us to say to ourselves:

'If I have only one life to live, let me live it as a proletarian, an Irishman (provided, of course, that I don't start out as Irish), a woman (if, similarly, I don't happen to be a woman), a European (from no particular European nation, naturally), or a proud member of the community of the deaf.' (Some of these desires will become clearer in due course.)

To the old question: 'Is there a ghost in the machine?' we can now answer: 'No, but there is a consumer.' The consumer selects his new identity from the vast range of moral possibilities that the modern world throws up. In its simplest form, the new identity is constructed by selecting one facet of someone's real given identity, and elevating it to the whole, or at least to a dominant part, of the personality. George Orwell forecast this process of reification in a 1948 review of Sartre's *Portrait of an Anti-Semite*:

> 'The' anti-Semite, he seems to imply all through the book, is always the same kind of a person, recognizable at a glance and, so to speak, in action the whole time. Actually one has only to use a little observation to see that anti-Semitism . . . in any but the worst cases, is intermittent. But [this] would not square with Monsieur Sartre's atomized vision of society. There is, he comes near to saying, no such thing as a human being, there are only different categories of men, such as 'the' worker, and 'the' bourgeois, all classifiable in much the same way as insects.*

A recent example of this kind of identity-building is the gay identity. For a gay is not simply a homosexual; he is someone who has made homosexuality the basis of an entire personality and outlook: morals, politics and social relations. This will tend to make him, or her, hostile to societies traditionally organized to favour heterosexuality and the family, and persuade him to advocate policies that seek not tolerance but the transformation of people's attitudes towards homosexuality.

Needless to say, this kind of response is by no means universal among homosexuals. Even today many homosexuals take the view that homosexuality is just one facet of their identity – whether an

* George Orwell, *The Collected Essays, Journalism and Letters*, Volume 4, *In Front of Your Nose 1945–1950*, Harmondsworth: Penguin Books, 1970, p. 510.

advantage, or a curse, or simply a slightly awkward fact about themselves – which has little bearing on the rest of their lives outside the bedroom. Their support for sexual reform will tend to go no further than social tolerance and the repeal of punitive laws. They may find the gay identity mysterious, alien, too narrow to express the full range of their personality, even repellent.

Here, in a passage from Noel Coward's diary, is the response of one such homosexual (by no means a repressed one) to the gay milieu of Fire Island in New York:

> I came back last night having spent Saturday and yesterday on Fire Island. I don't think I shall ever go again. It is lovely from the point of view of beach and sun and wearing no clothes, but the atmosphere is sick-sick-sick. Never in my life have I seen such concentrated abandoned homosexuality. It is fantastic and difficult to believe. I wished really that I hadn't gone. Thousands of queer young men of all shapes and sizes camping about blatantly and carrying on – in my opinion – appallingly. Then there were all the lesbians glowering at each other. Among this welter of brazen perversion wander a few 'straights', with children and dogs. I have always been of the opinion that a large group of queer men was unattractive. On Fire Island it is more than unattractive, it's macabre, sinister, irritating, and somehow tragic.

Let me briefly dispatch possible confusion between the idea of selecting one aspect of personality and elevating it to the status of a full identity, and the earlier point made by Bill and Shirley Letwin, that traditional identity can be modified by the reason's deciding to emphasize some aspects of one's environment at the expense of others. The difference between these two views is subtle but important and it has immense consequences. It is the difference between piecemeal self-improvement and the wholesale reconstruction of the personality. The person attempting piecemeal reform will usually refer to what he is doing in modest terms: 'I'm trying to be more punctual.' The person who is engaged in ideological reconstruction of himself will, appropriately enough, see it in dramatic, even religious terms, as a process of becoming a different sort of human being. He will be re-making himself in accordance with some revelation, either discovering his 'true' identity buried within himself, or discerning some new principle of truth outside himself to which he must conform, or some combination of the two. (See Kenneth Minogue's *Alien Powers*, passim.)

In such psychological revelations is identity politics born – usually on the Left – but not invariably. A striking example of magnifying part of an identity into the whole of one is the ideological definition of American identity to be found on the political Right – the claim that America is unlike other nations is that its nationality is not ethnic or cultural, but instead consists of allegiance to the principles of liberty and equality set out in the Declaration of Independence and embodied in the Constitution. To be sure, there is an ideological component in American nationality which the Declaration in particular dramatizes. (That is not, of course, unique to America; all nations which have played a part in world history as well as their own, notably the French, have furnished such ideological explanations of themselves.) But that ideology, important though it is, is merely the conscious political expression of a much more extensive national culture which is the result of the history, institutions, and the shared experience of living together in the same territory linked by communications.

An episode in the Second World War is instructive. During the Battle of the Bulge, German commandos were roaming around in American uniforms, and GIs seeking to establish the true identity of other soldiers asked questions to test their Americanism. Did they ask them their view of equality or rights of popular government? Of course not; mere ideas of that kind could be parroted – indeed, genuinely believed – by non-Americans. No, they asked them details of American life in the broadcast cultural context: the winner of the previous World Series, radio advertising jingles, the capital of their home state, Mae West's bust measurements. In short, the kinds of things that every American would know, but that a foreigner could not easily study. In his book *The Blood-Dimmed Time*, Gerald Astor describes how two Allied generals coped:

> General Omar Bradley said: 'Three times I was ordered to prove my identity by cautious GIs. The first time by identifying Springfield as the capital of Illinois (my questioner held out for

> Chicago); the second time by locating the guard between the centre and tackle on a line of scrimmage; the third time by naming the then-current spouse of a blonde called Betty Grable. Grable stopped me (the correct answer was bandleader Harry James) but the sentry did not. Pleased at having stopped me he . . . passed me on.
>
> General Montgomery . . . imperiously directed his driver to ignore the sentry. The guard shot out the tyres of his car and held the British commander for several hours. When he heard of the incident, Eisenhower enjoyed one of his few laughs during the Bulge . . .

In short, what shapes Americans and American national identity is the richness of the entire culture, not merely its conscious political expression.

But cannot someone become an American? And if so, does that not establish the validity of the idea of national identity (American national identity at least) as something to be chosen rather than merely accepted? That is certainly the view inherent in America's civic religion of itself and regularly intoned by judges who, when swearing in new United States citizens, assure them that they are every bit as American as the descendants of the Pilgrim Fathers. It is, however, a pious fallacy. A new United States citizen may have as many legal rights as a native-born American, but he has not been as shaped by the American experience. And if he has become an American out of sympathy for liberal principles, then his American identity will wax and wane in response to the course both of American history and of his own convictions. Suppose he changes his political views? Or America fails to live up to them? Very likely a consistent philosopher would be feeling twinges of disloyalty at the end of the first week.

A true version of becoming an American, as opposed to a United States citizen, would be that it is a process that is only realized in retrospect. A foreign resident who has married an American, brought up American children, lived an American life in all the everyday respects from school to supermarket, and worried through the nation's crises, will one day wake up to find that he has become an American. He will find himself unself-consciously using the pronoun 'we' when referring to Americans. No decision was necessary; no decision could have worked this transformation. Becoming an American is the same process for an immigrant as for a native-born child: living in America. United States citizenship is merely a legal ratification of this psychological evolution.

Once identity becomes a matter of choice or conscious decision, however, a rubicon has been crossed. For there are more radical ways of creating a new identity, whether sexual or national, than by over-emphasizing one aspect of one's given identity. One can over-emphasize an aspect of someone else's identity. Transsexualism, for instance, is an assertion that one can choose not merely to ape another sexual identity, but even to become a member of another sex. One can remake oneself, altered completely by surgery. This is a delusion, of course, since men who have surgically transformed themselves into make-believe women cannot, for instance, have children. The radical feminist Shulamith Firestone, however, advocates genetic engineering that will enable men and women to choose which sexual role – impregnation or child-bearing – they wish to undertake. Nature is no longer seen by such theorists as even a constraint upon identity because literally nothing is impossible for someone determined to be his own creator.

After all, to take another example, American bureaucrats have created an entire ethnic identity by a stroke of the pen. In 1973, in order to create a rational structure for affirmative action quotas, the Office of Management and Budget (OMB) promulgated Statistical Directive Number 13, as Michael Lind describes in *The Next American Nation*, dividing Americans into five ethnic groups of which the most creative is Hispanic. Now, Hispanics are not a national group; they include Cubans, Mexicans, Columbians, Chileans, even Spaniards. Nor are they a racial category, since they cover whites, blacks and Amerindians. Nor – and this is a surprise – are they even a linguistic category, because they include people with Spanish surnames from families who have not spoken Spanish for generations, or as in the case of some Mexican Amerindians, from families who have never spoken Spanish. But since being Hispanic has certain practical advantages – for instance, being the beneficiary of the quota spoils system, or receiving money from the Ford Foundation to advance Hispanic interests – there are now a considerable number of Americans, generally in academia but not exclusively so, who think of themselves as possessing the Hispanic identity. Indeed, as Linda Chavez pointed out, it is quite difficult for anyone with a Spanish surname to escape being educated in Spanish in the public schools, even if they cannot speak the language. The bureaucrats insist that they must be brought up, for the sake of their authentic identity, in their own culture – even though it is not their culture and, indeed, in so far as it is a hybrid-Hispanic culture, may not be anyone's culture, except possibly that of a Clinton cabinet appointee.

Can we see any common elements uniting these proliferating invented identities? Let me suggest three: First, they are stark and impoverished compared to 'given' identities; second, they are self-conscious and precarious; and third as Kenneth Minogue has pointed, they are the adversaries of traditional identities.

It goes almost without saying that an identity built upon one part of a personality will be impoverished alongside the richness of an identity which reflects the full range of influences upon a life. The Marxist categories of proletarian and bourgeois are useless except as economic categories. An identity based upon the fact that you work for wages and are alienated from the product of your labour is no identity at all. If a young Marxist intellectual were to ask for advice on how to live a good proletarian life, what advice would we give him? It would almost certainly not include, say, the breeding of racing pigeons, nor working an allotment, though both are important components of a genuine working-class life in Northern England.

Compare, on the other hand, the richness of the traditional social identity like that, for instance, of 'the gentleman'. As Shirley Letwin demonstrates in her book on *The Gentlemen in Trollope*, this is a subject yielding not only sharp and subtle social observations (and satires), but also a rich vein of moral criticism. One might say, in relation to today's topic, that the gentleman in Letwin is the highest example of moral reason operating to improve the personality from the material within it. False social identities, which tend to reconstruct the personality in accord with some ideal of reason from the outside, inevitably produce a one-dimensional man – the Soviet proletarian, an examination of whose moral character can sustain nothing more complicated than a cartoon or a socialist-realist painting (which is hard to distinguish from a cartoon). In addition to being thin, invented identities are also extremely precarious.

The more natural our identity is, the more we take it for granted. Self-consciousness is the constant companion of uncertainty. We are self-conscious on entering the room at someone else's party, conscious of other people's needs and enjoyment when we give a party at home. A good example of self-consciousness as the attribute of an uncertain identity occurs in Thomas Mann's *Felix Krull*. Krull is travelling in a comfortable first-class train compartment, to all intents and purposes a young aristocrat. As a train attendant is leaving his compartment, Krull smiles at him: 'that assuredly confirmed him in his conservative principles to the point where he would gladly have fought and died for them.' The point, however, is that Krull is not a young aristocrat; he is a confidence trickster. It is extremely doubtful that a real aristocrat would react in this way. He would simply be less conscious of his impact, flaunting his identity only when expected marks of deference were not paid to him. But the confidence man has to calculate such effects with precision, because his hold on an aristocratic identity is extremely precarious.

Hence the phenomenon of the marginal patriot – the outsider who seeks to demonstrate his commitment to, say, a national identity by being more nationalistic than thou. John Stephenson, a Paddington-born man of uncertain ancestry, thus became Sean MacStiofain, the chief of staff of the IRA in the 1970s. MacStiofain succeeded heroically, or rather anti-heroically, in his identity as an Irish patriot, going so far as to launch a hunger strike. Near death, however, he gave up the strike, at which point his IRA colleagues suddenly realized he had been an Englishman all along. His Irish identity had always been precarious; it depended upon his performing heroic feats.

Another instance is the eagerness with which gays greet any scientific work which suggests that homosexuality may be rooted in the genes. In theory, they need not worry about the tyranny of nature in relation to sexual identity. 'Queer theory' is supposed to have established that gender is 'socially constructed'. Yet they give an almost desperate endorsement to the authority of science and nature when that seems likely to support the inevitability of the identity that appeals to them.

But the single most significant characteristic of the invented identity is that it is both parasite and adversary towards the real thing. An invented identity, as we have seen, will model itself on an existing one. Gay families mimic traditional families by copying the parental role and demanding such rights as pension rights for domestic partners. But they are unable to perform important aspects of the role, such as child-bearing, and they are often unwilling to accept its disciplines, such as sexual fidelity. Similarly, invented national identities copy the outward shell of real nations. For instance the European Union is gradually acquiring a flag, an anthem, citizenship and even an army without the prior substance of a single people with a sense of community and allegiance.

These imitations naturally weaken the real identities, whether of family or of nation, by sucking the significance out of the forms and practices that traditionally bolster them. If, for instance, unofficial and transient relationships have their financial arrangements underpinned by the state, then the family derives no special significance from the fact that its own arrangements are similarly protected.

But the hostility of the invented identity goes beyond this parasitism. As Professor Minogue has pointed out in *Alien Powers*, the first impulse of someone who has thrown off his old identity and embraced a new one is an evangelical impulse. He wants to tell everyone that once he was blind, that now he sees, but that they are still blind. And what he sees is that his old identity was a fraud and an imposition, and that their current identity still is. Hence, new identities tend to attack and seek to replace their counterparts among existing identities. Thus the gay or feminist identity will define itself by opposition to the traditional sexual identities of male and female. These it will decry as socially constructed and consequently false and oppressive 'heterosexism' in the jargon.

In the case of national identities, the rivalry between ideological nationalisms – analysed with such devastating irony by Elie Kedourie in his classic *Nationalism* – and taken-for-granted ethnocultural nationalisms can be especially vicious. For pre-existing loyalties are an obstacle to the new national identity that is striving to be born. And since ideological nationalists act upon Charles Stewart Parnell's principle that 'No man has the right to fix the boundary of the march of a nation . . .', the opposition may legitimately face extirpation –

sometimes literally: real people and real peoples were murdered in the campaign to create a new Soviet man.

At other times, ideological nationalism leads to polemics rather than to Golgotha. Thus the Canadian nationalist identity – the officially fostered and bilingual one, manufactured in Ottawa – defines itself by a hostility to the actual nationalisms of Quebec and English Canada, particularly the latter since it is the nationalism of the majority. It is also hostile to the seductive English-speaking American identity next door; the first claim of a Canadian nationalist is that he is 'not American'. Euro-nationalism in Brussels is constantly engaged in polemics against its rivals, the traditional patriotisms of France, Britain and other European countries which it blames for past wars, racism, and all the fashionable vices.

And in the United States, the theory that America is a nation of immigrants held together only by allegiance to liberal political ideas is not only in a state of constant tension with the actual American historical identity for it implies that America is the whole world in microcosm, that everyone is in principle an American, and that therefore America's English-speaking culture is merely the property of an ethnic group or a temporary majority. Hence it is now the carrier of multiculturalism. This theory holds that America is a constitutional umbrella sheltering not individuals but the ethnocultural identities of Anglos, Hispanics, blacks, etc. Ideological Americanism thereby helps to deconstruct America in the most literal sense by making it a loose federation of cultural identities. The parable of the Tower of Babel might have been invented to describe this progress from hubris to incoherence.

What does all this matter? One might in theory suppose that a theory of identity as infinitely plastic, a succession of masks chosen in response to the applause of the others as much as for the satisfaction of one's (hypothetical) self, would lead to social peace. After all, have not conflicts until now been clashes between the hard and supposedly unyielding identities of nation, class and ethnicity? Surely a widespread acceptance of the malleability of identity would lead to a tolerance of other identities as equally valid (or bogus) as one's own, perhaps even to the construction of a supra-identity of tolerance within which all these identity sub-cultures could comfortably coexist – a kind of Austria–Hungary of moral visions in which the ruling power demands only the mildest of allegiances, one easily compatible with the identity's integrity.

Alas, it does not seem to be working out that way. Social conflict between different groups seems to be multiplying in lockstep with the increased popularity of the theory of malleable identity and with the expansion of university studies in gender, class, gayness, ethnicity, etc.

Is this increase in social conflict related to the concept of identity as plastic? A plastic identity is, in principle, arbitrary and limitless. There is literally no group, however arbitrarily selected, which cannot conceive of itself as possessing a specific 'identity' and thus forming a particular 'community'. The number of groups which claim some such basis for affiliation are multiplying rapidly. The late Aaron Wildavsky once calculated, tongue in cheek, that groups of this kind, including women, blacks, Eskimos, Hispanics and the disabled, added up to more than 300 per cent of the American people.

Even the process of expansion can sometimes provoke conflict when some members of a group don't want to share in the proffered identity and the group seeks to bring them into line. The outing of private homosexuals by gay activists is just such a conflict that arises when identity becomes a cause rather than a given fact. Still more extreme, the 'deaf community' in the United States imagines itself to be a self-conscious community with its own language, culture and identity. Spokesmen for its organization, the National Association for the Deaf, denounce attempts to enable the deaf to hear as cultural genocide (I am not making this up). They have even lobbied the federal government to prevent parents of deaf children from relieving their deafness through an operation that surgically installs a hearing device in a child's head and allows him to develop normal hearing and speech skills. (I should, in all honesty, add that the chairman of the study group that made this recommendation is not himself deaf.)

More significantly, identity is not just how we feel about ourselves; to be truly satisfying, our identity needs to be recognized by others. Yet imagine how difficult it must be for some of the groups now in existence to be treated as possessing true identities by the rest of society. For instance, there is 'the S & M Community'. This is a group of sadists and masochists who in New York have formed the Eulenspiegel Society and meet in various night-clubs with names like 'the Dungeon'. In an absolutely wonderful paradox, they complain that they are oppressed by society by being forced to conceal their lifestyles. Indeed the Eulenspiegel Society was originally founded in 1971 as a 'masochists' rights' group (*New York Magazine*, 28 November 1994). Sadists were admitted later – doubtless the first expression of the rights the society exists to protect.

Such forms of identity politics promise long-running cultural wars. There is little prospect that most people, even those privately attracted to these sexual practices, will ever be prepared to grant any sort of respectable social status, let along official standing, to the Eulenspiegel Society and similar groups. But they will continue to push for recognition, legal and otherwise. An organization of paedophiles did manage to get itself recognized, first, as a non-governmental organization by the United Nations through its membership in a larger gay coalition, and subsequently as a tax-exempt educational group in its own right. These caused political rows, and its UN accreditation was later withdrawn. But we may expect the demand for recognition by this and similar groups to be renewed.

And when the demand is resisted, or even when it is conceded without enthusiasm, the disappointed group will seek to force a deeper acceptance from others. As John Gray has pointed out, tolerance is no longer enough for such groups because it implies that the thing tolerated merits disapproval. And disapproval will seem especially insulting when a question of identity is at stake. If a practice someone performs or a belief he holds excites disapproval, he may be wounded or privately bitter. If his very identity excites disapproval, then he will become outraged and demand a more substantive surrender by his critics, perhaps even the repression of their objections ('hate speech'). In this context, you might say that the paedophiles want to make us cry 'Uncle'. They are a long way from success as yet. But the larger gay community has been quite successful in transforming the moral disapproval of it critics into a medical-cum-psychological disorder called 'homophobia', the main symptom of which is being accused of it.

What, finally, maximizes the likelihood of conflict is that the refusal to extend approval may be implicit in some other identity. Even the most multicultural feminist can extend tolerance, let alone approval, to an Islamic identity because of its hostility to women's education. Similarly, the Afro-centrist or Hispanic activist is bound to reject the political arrangements and electoral boundaries based upon a non-racial or monocultural concept of American identity. Hence, in numberless ways, the multiplication of chosen identities leads to endless social conflict.

When modern psychologists and modernist writers began deconstructing what they thought was the prison of a rigid and unreflecting identity, they doubtless thought they were liberating the citizens to stroll about in free and equal relationships without bumping into the barriers of race, gender, ethnicity and class. What they were in fact doing was laying the epistemological ground for low-intensity civil war.

III

CONSERVATIVE REALISM AND CHRISTIAN DEMOCRACY

NOEL MALCOLM

'Realism' is not a technical term in political theory (except in the field of international relations). Even if it were, all politicians would claim that it applied in some way or other to them. The obvious contrast is between realism and idealism; but those who claim to be idealistic about their ends will also insist that they are realists when it comes to the question of means. Since conservatives do not claim to be idealists anyway, the phrase 'conservative realism' may seem like a redundant duplication of terms. I believe that, nevertheless, it can be properly used to suggest a strand of conservative thinking, a set of attitudes, an area of concerns.

Most attempts to describe the nature of conservatism depend heavily on negative arguments. Conservatism is not utopian; it rejects rationalism; it is anti- or non-'scientific' (in the sense in which socialism claims to be scientific); it distrusts state planning, and so on. After a long string of such negative descriptions, the listener may be left with the impression that conservatism is little more than the politics of inertia, hesitancy or doubt. Conservatives are sometimes depicted as blind defenders of the status quo, believers in the principle that whatever is, is right. Or, by extension, they are seen as nursing a romanticism of the past – the politics of social or cultural nostalgia.

'Conservative realism' suggests otherwise. It implies that conservatives can be realistic, not just in their sceptical view of human nature, but in their appreciation of economic realities and in their understanding of the nature of political action. It has overtones of a tougher, more hard-headed and more active exercise of political power, both nationally and internationally. In the policies of the British Conservative government during the 1980s, two areas in particular merited the use of the term 'conservative realism'. The first was the attempt to force through a recognition of economic realities: monetarist methods to control inflation, supply-side economics to remove brakes and distortions in the supply of labour, and a constant insistence on the laws of the market, the discipline of competition and the inherent dynamism of a properly functioning capitalist economy. The second area in which 'conservative realism' was displayed was that of the defence of national interests on the international stage – a defence conducted by all means possible, including, in the early 1980s, military force. The very idea that the reality of international politics consists of a competition between national interests made the British government sceptical of any plans to submerge national interests in supranational entities such as the European Community.

These two distinctive features of Margaret Thatcher's policy became the two principal bugbears of her critics. The economic reforms were denounced as rampant individualism, the politics of greed and selfishness. The defence of national interests, together with the scepticism shown towards supranational projects, were denounced as blind nationalism or xenophobia. Outside the Conservative Party, such criticisms were of course made without reserve. Inside the party, however, a certain element of indirection, even of code, was necessary in order to convey criticisms of this kind. On the question of moderating or reversing some of the Thatcherite economic reforms, some appeal was made to so-called 'One Nation' Toryism; but this was a term with an awkwardly specific historical content, referring most immediately to a group of politicians in the 1960s which had actually included Enoch Powell, the John the Baptist of monetarist policy. In any case, the appeal to 'One Nation' was not obviously in tune with the other main current of anti-Thatcherite feeling, namely, the dislike of her robust defence of the nation-state in Europe. Some other code was needed.

For some of the non-Thatcherites in Mrs Thatcher's government, it was Europe itself that provided the answer. In the generation of clever young men who had risen rapidly through the Conservative Party machine under the patronage of Edward Heath, there were several who had campaigned hard for British membership of the European Community and, in the process, had acquired friends and ideological allies on the Continent. David Hunt, who was one of the

Thatcher government's senior whips and became a Minister of State for the Environment in 1989, had led an Anglo-German political youth movement in the 1970s (a grouping of British Conservatives and German Christian Democrats) which had pressed for greater European integration. Chris Patten, who had held four different ministerial posts under Mrs Thatcher before becoming Chairman of the Party in 1990, had been a strong defender of Edward Heath's European policy in the early 1970s; in addition, his devout Catholicism gave him a special reason for taking an interest in those European political parties whose philosophy was explicitly linked to the traditions of Catholic social doctrine.

For Conservative politicians such as these, it was natural to look towards German Christian Democrats, or Christian Democracy in general, as a more appealing model of what the British Conservative Party might do or be. To praise the Christian Democrats was, in a coded way, to criticize precisely those aspects of recent British government policy which the non-Thatcherites disliked. Christian Democrats, while accepting the basic principles of capitalism and the market, insisted on high levels of 'social protection', favoured worker participation in the management of industry, and generally cultivated a political language in which terms such as 'solidarity', 'partnership' and 'consensus' figured prominently. And at the same time the Christian Democrat parties on the Continent were, and had long been, the leading proponents of ever closer European integration.

A particularly favourable opportunity for drawing attention to these Christian Democrat principles arose during the last years of Mrs Thatcher's government because of developments in the European Parliament at Strasbourg. The biggest groupings of national parties had, for many years, been the Socialist Group and the group of Christian Democrats (which called itself the European People's Party). The British Conservatives belonged to a third, much smaller, alliance, called the European Democratic Group; its other members were a handful of Danes and Spaniards. In 1989 the Spaniards announced that they were planning to join the Christian Democrat group instead, and the Danish contingent was reduced at the elections from four to two. At this point it was agreed that, in order to play a more effective role in countering the now dominant Socialist Group, the entire Anglo-Spanish-Danish grouping would apply to join the group of Christian Democrat parties, at least on an arm's-length arrangement known as 'allied membership'. (The British Conservatives could not become full members of the group, because only parties whose programmes or statutes make explicit reference to Christian values can do so.) Negotiations over this dragged on through 1989 and 1990; it was eventually agreed that the Conservatives would be allowed to join the Christian Democrats as allied members in 1992. During this process, there were many opportunities for Conservative politicians to emphasize all the ways in which they thought their party might benefit, ideologically as well as pragmatically, from a closer association with the Christian Democrats. Further impetus in this direction came after the fall of Mrs Thatcher, when one of John Major's earliest foreign policy initiatives was an attempt to construct a closer political relationship with Chancellor Kohl's Christian Democrat German government.

The first sign that 'Christian Democracy' might be the by-word for a new, post-Thatcherite and non-Thatcherite type of Conservatism came from a likely speaker in an unlikely place. In a long interview in the pages of *Marxism Today*, Chris Patten set out his Christian Democrat stall.

> What I think is that if we can find, more successfully than we've been able to in the past, an English rhetoric for what seems to come so naturally to the German Christian Democrats, namely the social market economy, then we're onto a very substantial winner . . . I say that because there is a feeling that while we need to continue to apply some of the economic lessons that we've been attempting to learn in the 1980s, there's also a feeling that we need to be more explicit about the social responsibilities that should go with successful individualism . . . If you were to put round the table Volker Ruhe and one or two of his colleagues in the German CDU, and Ken Clarke, John Gummer, Tony Newton, and others, and me, . . . you'd often be hard-pressed to know which was which . . . I find myself very much at home talking to German Christian Democrats.*

Unfortunately, Mr Patten lost his seat at the next election, and was

* Chris Patten, 'The Power to Change' (interview with David Marquand), in *Marxism Today*, Feb. 1991, pp. 20–3.

subsequently translated to Hong Kong. The torch of Christian Democracy has been held aloft, however, by David Hunt, who for some time enjoyed high ministerial office in the Major governments. Mr Hunt has returned to this theme in several of his speeches, and above all in an important pamphlet published by the Conservative Political Centre in March 1994:

> My own background in politics is a very European one, and I have always sought out common ground between European Christian Democracy and the institutions and traditions of British Conservatism. When Volker Ruhe, now the German Defence Minister, and I led the European Christian Democratic and Conservative Youth Community 20 years ago, we were both determined to lay the foundations for a deeper understanding of our common political philosophy ... We sell ourselves short if, paraphrasing the Bolsheviks of the 1920s, we reconcile ourselves to 'Conservatism in one country' ... Christian Democrats elsewhere in Western Europe – and the Church in Western Europe – have very significant common ground with what we recognize here as Conservatism: in supporting the principles of the *market economy*, and in supporting subsidiarity.*

Such claims about the close affinity between Conservatism and European Christian Democracy have surfaced from time to time in British political debate during the last four years; but it would be fair to say that this theme has never become really dominant. One reason for this may be the open disagreement between Christian Democratic proposals for a fully federal European constitution and the much more cautious official policy of the British government. (During the 1994 European election, for example, the British Foreign Secretary had to insist testily at several press conferences that the Conservatives, as mere 'allied members', were not bound by the EPP's election manifesto.)

But there may be a more basic reason why the much-trumpeted ideological betrothal between Conservatism and Christian Democracy has never been consummated. Quite simply, most politicians

* David Hunt, *Right Ahead: Conservatism and the Social Market*, London, 1994, pp. 13–15.

and commentators in Britain have very little idea what Christian Democracy really stands for. There is not a single straightforward modern textbook in English devoted to the history and principles of Christian Democracy; the standard work, by Michael Fogarty, is now nearly forty years out of date.* And those general textbooks which do attempt, in passing, to characterize modern Christian Democracy give very contradictory accounts of it. Some do indeed treat it as a variant of conservatism: Lane and Ersson say that 'in many cases it is difficult to distinguish conservative parties from Christian Democrat parties', and Steiner describes the Christian Democrats merely as conservatives who include the word 'Christian' in their name.** Others, however, portray Christian Democracy as a 'centre party' phenomenon, with a specifically anti-liberal (in the nineteenth-century economic sense of 'liberal') ideology.*** Michael Fogarty, the leading British analyst of Christian Democratic politics in the post-war period, had no hesitation in declaring that 'all Christian Democrat parties' belonged 'essentially to the Centre'.†

The range of possibilities is wider than that, however. Looking through the history of the main post-war Christian Democrat parties in Europe, one can find plenty of evidence to suggest that Christian Democracy is compatible with policies, and electoral strategies, of the left. One senior Italian Christian Democrat described his party's political strategy in the 1970s as follows: 'We strive to work with the other forces of the left, the Socialists and, if you want, the Communists, to bring about reform and democracy.'†† A famous definition of French Christian Democrat political action was given by Georges Bidault, the former French foreign minister, who said: 'To govern in the centre, and pursue, by the methods of the right, the policies

* M. P. Fogarty, *Christian Democracy in Western Europe, 1820–1953*, London, 1957.

** J.-E. Lane and S. O. Ersson, *Politics and Society in Western Europe*, London, 1991, p. 108; J. Steiner, *European Democracies*, London, 1986, p. 30; these citations are taken from K. van Keesbergen, 'The Distinctiveness of Christian Democracy', in D. Hanley (ed.), *Christian Democracy in Europe: A Comparative Perspective*, London, 1994, pp. 31–47; here p. 32.

*** *Ibid.*, pp. 34–5.

† Fogarty, op. cit., p. 333.

†† An anonymous leader of the 'Base' faction of the party, quoted in A. S. Zuckerman, *The Politics of Faction: Christian Democrat Rule in Italy*, New Haven, 1979, p. 114.

of the left.'* It is hardly surprising that some analysts, faced with this conflicting and bewildering evidence, have concluded that the Christian Democrat parties do not in fact express any coherent set of political principles, and are best described on as 'catch-all' parties.** Not for nothing, it seems, was the German CDU described in its first decade as little more than a *Kanzlerwahlverein*, a wide-ranging but ad hoc association of people brought together only by their support for a common candidate for the Chancellorship.*** One commentator, considering the range of political positions gathered together in the CDU and CSU immediately after the war, declared: 'This party is socialist and radical in Berlin, clerical and conservative in Cologne, capitalist and reactionary in Hamburg and counter-revolutionary and particularistic in Munich.†

In order to see how it was that these different and sometimes contradictory strands of opinion could be woven together in a single political movement, it is necessary to look briefly at the historical development of Christian Democracy in Europe. Christian Democracy has never been a simple, unitary thing; but that does not mean that it has no defining or distinguishing features whatsoever. It is a complex product of two things: a history of political activity on the one hand, and a body of theory on the other. That body of theory, although strongly linked to a doctrinal tradition which claims to express timeless truths, has itself also been influenced by modern political history.

The coming together of democratic politics and Christian (mainly, Catholic) beliefs occurred in most continental European countries during the nineteenth century. The growth of mass politics, or at least the extension of representative democracy, could not fail to interact with a Church which bore pastoral responsibilities for the masses, and increasingly felt the need to reclaim or re-evangelize the inhabitants of the rapidly expanding industrial cities. At the same

* Hans Maier, *Revolution and Church: The Early History of Christian Democracy, 1789–1901*, tr. E. M. Schlossberger, Notre Dame, 1969, p. 9.

** Van Keesbergen, *op. cit.*, pp. 34–5.

*** G. Pridham, 'Christian Democracy in Italy and West Germany: A Comparative Analysis', in M. Kolinsky and W. E. Paterson (eds), *Social and Political Movements in Western Europe*, London, 1976, pp. 142–74; here p. 146.

† Quoted in Pridham, *op. cit.*, p. 153.

time, the growth in the powers and responsibilities of the State, and its increasing assumption of control over matters such as education and poor relief, led to frequent clashes between Church and State. Broadly speaking, then, there were two main ways in which Christians (usually Catholics) could become involved in democratic politics: one defensive, the other, so to speak, offensive. On the one hand, groups of Catholic activists could enter the political system in order to defend the interests of the Church, or to preserve its values from policies which undermined them. (The classic example of this was the Zentrum party of Germany, which led the resistance to Bismarck in the political arena during the *Kulturkampf* of the 1870s.) On the other hand, Catholics could go out and form political movements – and engage in other types of quasi-political activity, such as organizing trade unions – because such political instruments offered an opportunity for spreading the values and beliefs of the Church more widely among the population. This approach naturally involved taking the social and economic problems of mass society as essential political issues, and accepting the idea that their amelioration, through the means supplied by modern representative politics, was itself fully compatible with Christian teaching – or, indeed, a fulfilment of it.

Both of these approaches (self-defence on the one hand, socio-political *reconquista* on the other) could veer off into more extreme forms. On the Catholic right, especially among clericalist intellectuals and socially conservative land-owners, there was always a tendency to believe that the democratic State was, by its very nature, inimical to the Church and Christian values. In France and Italy, such people were likely to join so-called 'intransigent' movements in the years before the First World War, and in some cases to end up as supporters of *Action Française* or Mussolini's Fascist movement.

At the other extreme, on the Catholic left, there were radical clericals who believed that the social and economic emancipation of the labouring classes was a positive dictate of Christian theology: as Frédéric Ozanam put it in the mid-1840s, 'we must go over to the side of the barbarians'. The term 'social justice' was developed during this period as a way of suggesting that social reforms and the redistribution of wealth were not just matters for charity, but absolute dictates of Christian ethics. 'Christian Socialism' came to the fore in 1848, and its leading French exponent, Philippe Buchez, was briefly President of the Republic. But holding political power was a very exceptional experience for such people. Usually they were peripheral critics of a political machinery which they could not control: like contemporary socialists of other varieties, they saw the so-called democratic state as an apparatus of power in the hands of vested bourgeois interests.

At either extreme, there were reasons for rejecting the modern democratic political system as such. It was between those extremes, therefore, that Catholic activists, for a mixture of self-defensive and pastoral reasons, could create that fusion of theological principles and democratic methods which came to be known as Christian Democracy.

Of all the factors which helped to bring that fusion about, the most important was the concern for matters of social policy shown by Pope Leo XIII. His encyclical letter *Rerum Novarum*, issued in 1891, was the first of the great modern series of papal encyclicals dealing with social and political questions. English translations of this text are sometimes printed under the title *On the Condition of the Workers*, and this is an apt reflection of the encyclical's contents. Leo XIII was deeply worried by the poverty of the labouring classes in Europe's industrial cities ('those', as he put it, 'whose cause we are pleading'), and insisted that the Church, although concerned ultimately with their spiritual welfare, could not ignore their temporal condition either. While he criticized the liberal economics which had appeared to justify the pushing down of labourers' wages, he was even more hostile towards the principles of socialism (by which he meant what we would broadly call communism): one might almost say that the purpose of *Rerum Novarum* was to save society from socialism by showing that, using social policies inspired by Catholic teaching, the discontents of the working classes could be gradually assuaged. Against the socialists, he insisted that the right to hold private property was fundamental to human society, and that this right must therefore be upheld by law. Christian ethics demanded charity towards the poor, of course; but Leo XIII distinguished carefully between ethics and law. Citing Christ's instruction 'Give alms from what you have' (Luke XI.41), he commented: 'These are not duties of justice, except in extreme cases, but of Christian charity, duties which it is not right to have enforced by law.*

Overall, indeed, this encyclical represented a rejection of the whole theory of 'social justice': the main influences on Leo's thinking here were the French paternalist Catholic activists led by René de La Tour du Pin and Léon Harmel, who saw social reform as essentially an expression of charity, and the Italian theorist Giuseppe Toniolo, whose social and economic thinking was based on an idealization of the guild system of Renaissance Florence, which he saw as an embodiment of medieval Christian teaching about social harmony. The main emphasis of *Rerum Novarum* was on the promotion of voluntary associations, such as Catholic trade unions; but it also contained passages about the concept of a 'just wage', and general defences of the right of the State to intervene in order to protect the interests of the poorest members of society. These and other arguments, to which I shall return in the final part of this chapter, gave rise to a mass of theoretical ambiguities, which later developments in Catholic teaching and Christian Democrat practice would only deepen and intensify.

Nevertheless, the immediate implications of *Rerum Novarum* were quite straightforward: Catholics could and should engage in projects of social reform, and their activities could be channelled not only into voluntary associations, but also through the political machinery of the state itself. This last aspect of papal teaching was specifically encouraged in France, where Leo gave his backing to the idea of *ralliement*, the rallying to the Republic. And so it was that in 1896 Léon Harmel organised the *Parti Démocrate Chrétien*, the first political party to use the term 'Christian Democrat' in its title. The general project of this party was to bring the masses back to the Church, improving their economic conditions in the process, and thereby to revive a society based on Christian principles. Unfortunately, however, the party was quickly thrown back into a more defensive posture of trying to protect Catholic institutional interests during France's own *Kulturkampf*. A similar problem beset the first Italian Christian Democrat party, organized by a young priest, Don Romolo Murri,

* *Rerum Novarum* para. 21, in M. Walsh and B. Davies (eds), *Proclaiming Justice and Peace: Documents from John XXIII to John Paul II*, London, 1991.

in 1898. (Because of the still unresolved conflict between the Papacy and the new Italian State, the freedom of action of Murri's party was particularly constricted: Catholics were in fact still forbidden by the Pope to vote in national elections.) In France, meanwhile, the Parti Démocrate Chrétien became entangled in an alliance with the anti-Dreyfusards, and performed very badly in the 1898 elections.

Considering these developments, Leo XIII realized that for one political party to arrogate the name 'Christian' to itself might actually be an obstacle to the general Christianizing of the political system. In 1901 he issued a stern encyclical, *Graves de communi*, in which for the first time the term 'Christian Democracy' was itself mentioned and defined. 'It is wrong,' he wrote, 'to twist the term "Christian Democracy" into something political. For although the term "democracy", in the meaning assigned to it by the philosophers, denotes rule by the people; nevertheless in the matter presently under discussion it should be taken in such a way that, leaving aside all political notions, the only meaning it conveys is that of beneficial Christian action among the people.'* This encyclical had a profound effect on Catholic politics; until the terms of it were altered by Pius XII in 1944, most Christian Democrats usually adopted the formula 'democrats of Christian inspiration' instead.

For nearly two decades after the promulgation of *Graves de communi*, most Christian Democrat activity was confined to non-party organizations. The most important of these in France was the *Sillon* (or 'furrow') movement, led by the charismatic Marc Sangnier, whose declared aim was 'to live Catholicism individually and collectively': when this was broken up by Pius X in 1910 and placed under the direct control of local bishops, Sangnier then founded a quasi-party, the *Ligue de la Jeune République*, which called for 'politics without politicians'. In Italy the intellectual leader of non-party Christian Democracy during this period was a young Sicilian priest, Don Luigi Sturzo, who became head of the lay 'Catholic Action' movement.

Two important factors contributed to the development of twentieth-century 'Christian Democrat' parties as we know them. One was this period of enforced distancing between Catholic social acti-

* *Acta sanctae sedis*, vol. 33 (1900–1901), pp. 385–96; here p. 387 (my translation).

vists and party politics, which enabled them to detach themselves from the 'clericalist' defence of Catholic institutional interests. The other was the First World War and its political aftermath, by which a new political landscape was created in many European countries. In Italy, Sturzo set up the Partito Popolare, which helped to block the socialists in the 1919 election, and entered into a loose collaboration with Giolitti's Liberals; in 1922, however, it helped to create the political deadlock which enabled Mussolini to come to power. The Partito Popolare was a genuine political party, in the sense that although it had the official approval of the Vatican when it was set up, it was not directly controlled by the institutions of the Church. At the same time, it had an excessively loose and general political character; one modern study describes it as 'a vast catch-all party'.* Its general aim was democratic reform, and its one particular purpose was the promotion of peasant smallholdings. Pius XI, who became Pope in 1922, regarded its general reformist character with suspicion, and helped to undermine it during the following three years. First he supported the removal of Sturzo from the leadership and his replacement by de Gasperi; then, when de Gasperi tried to form a 'Centrist' coalition with moderate socialists to oppose Mussolini, the Pope condemned the idea of any such collaboration. The party was then closed down by Mussolini in the following year.

In Germany, the Zentrum party remained weak and ill-organized during the Weimar years. With its continuous history dating from the *Kulturkampf*, it remained not so much a Catholic reform party as a party for the defence of Catholic interests: at most, it was 'a loose collection of Catholic regional and socio-economic interest groups'.** It eventually voted for Hitler's enabling law, and was dissolved thereafter.

France, meanwhile, had seen the birth of a new party comparable to the Italian Partito Popolare: this was the Parti Démocrate Populaire, founded in 1924. Calling itself a centre party, and describing its programme as 'a synthesis of what is just in the programmes of the Right and Left', it concentrated on proposals for constitutional

* R. A. Webster, *The Cross and the Fasces: Christian Democracy and Fascism in Italy, 1860–1960*, Stanford University Press, 1968, p. 63.

** A. J. Heidenheimer, *Adenauer and the CDU: The Rise of the Leader and the Integration of the Party*, The Hague, 1960, p. 8.

reform such as women's suffrage, proportional representation, and replacing the Senate with a quasi-corporativist upper chamber representing professions, family interests, and so on. Its leadership discussed the idea of collaborating with socialists and communists, but in the end decided against it. Strengthened by the Pope's condemnation of *Action Française* in 1926, it continued to play an active role in French politics throughout the inter-war years; however, it never became a mass party, attracting on average 3 per cent of the national vote.

More important for the development of French Christian Democratic thinking during these years was the growth of non-party movements devoted to Catholic social and political thought – the heirs, in effect, of Sangnier's *Sillon* movement – of which the *Esprit* movement, founded and led by the philosopher Emmanuel Mounier in the 1930s, was by far the most significant. Mounier kept his distance from the Parti Démocrate Populaire, and indeed criticized the whole existing system of liberal democratic politics as part of the problem (what he called 'the established disorder') to which the only true solution would be a pre-political revival of moral and spiritual values among the population as a whole.

The sense that the entire Western political and economic system was structurally unsound was of course intensified by the economic crisis of the early 1930s. And in 1931 this way of looking at things received some support from the Pope, Pius XI, who issued the second of the great encyclicals on social and political affairs, *Quadragesimo anno*. Condemning, with symmetrical disdain, 'socialism' on the one hand and 'individualism' on the other, Pius XI called for a spiritual regeneration of society. But in rejecting both the class struggle which the socialists called for and the free play of market forces which the capitalists appeared to defend, the Pope was drawn towards recommending a new form of socio-economic organization, a corporativist system in which both employers and employed would be contained in and represented by the same bodies. This idea, which stemmed originally from the corporativist 'guild'-theory of Professor Toniolo, came uncomfortably close to the corporativism currently being developed by Mussolini's own theoreticians.

Quadragesimo anno was indeed hailed by Fascist theorists, such as Father Gemelli of the Catholic University of Milan, as an endorsement of Mussolini's system. One work used as a textbook in Italian schools during the 1930s, Amintore Fanfani's *Il Significato del corporativismo*, explained that the forms of state intervention developed by Mussolini 'bring out the profound moral character of the Fascist corporative doctrine and rightly approach, in these demands, the doctrine on the use of goods which the Catholic Church has been preaching for centuries'.* (It is a little unfortunate that Mr David Hunt, in his urge to display the intellectual respectability of the Christian Democratic tradition, should have chosen to quote in his pamphlet from precisely this work by Fanfani, apparently unaware of the murky pre-war past of this famous post-war Christian Democrat politician.) In Germany, similarly, there were attempts to show that Christian Democrats could support the Nazi programme. In a broadcast address to German Catholics in 1934, von Papen announced: 'Everywhere we view a happy harmony and full agreement between the demands of *Quadragesimo anno* and National Socialist policies . . . The Third Reich, under Hitler, is the first state in the world in which the sublime principles of the popes have . . . been put into practice.**

Politically, the overall history of Christian Democracy during the inter-war years is one of failure – albeit a failure in the face of overwhelming odds. Some of the blame must be attached to the interference of the papacy under Pius XI, who both weakened the Christian Democrat parties politically and burdened them with an over-specific recommendation of one particular (and particularly dubious) form of socio-economic organization. It is tempting to say that the Christian Democrat parties really needed to be left alone to function as ordinary political parties. But, on the other hand, without some specific guidance from above, it was not obvious how they could retain a programme and a character distinctive enough to justify their continued separate existence – as their unsteady political trajectory, drifting in and out of alliances with liberal, right-wing and left-wing forces, suggests. So long as the Christian Democrats were concerned with defending the interests of the Church, as many of their leaders were in the earliest phases of the movement's history, they did at least have the makings of a political programme or position. But as

* Webster, *op. cit.*, p. 158.
** Heidenheimer, *op. cit.*, p. 15.

that institutional rationale dropped away, they were left with an unstable mixture of two things: opportunist practical politics in a merry-go-round of electoral alliances on the one hand, and an airy theoretical disdain for the very nature of adversarial politics on the other. This political stance of 'anti-politics' was easily combined with the anti-capitalist rhetoric of Pius XI, to produce an attitude of hostility towards the basic institutions of the modern liberal-democratic State: such an attitude was, unfortunately, not altogether dissimilar from some elements of Fascist ideology, even though many Christian Democrats did, of course, remain strongly opposed to Fascism in practice. 'Anti-politics' politics, which in post-war Europe has been associated mainly with the centre-left (for example, in the anti-adversarial claims of the SDP in 1980s Britain, or in the technocratic ideals of the European movement founded by Monnet), was part of the armoury of Fascist ideology in the inter-war period.

It was only after Fascism had been defeated in war that Europe was able to experience the rebirth of Christian Democracy as a political phenomenon. Some of those who helped to form the new Christian Democrat parties did have distinguished records as opponents of the Fascist or Nazi regimes, and in Italy especially the party could draw on a large pool of non-communist resistance fighters. The horrors of the war made an appeal to basic Christian values a reassuring foundation for any political revival. Alignment on the side of Britain and the United States had also encouraged some influential politicians and thinkers (above all, Jacques Maritain in America) to identify Christian values much more unequivocally with the ideas of representative democracy and universal human rights than they had done previously. The old conservative, liberal and centre parties had crumbled or collapsed; and in both Italy and Germany there was an awareness that socialists or even communists might come to power unless a broad grouping of non-left-wing democrats could quickly be established to block them. At the same time, the experience of Fascism had discredited any talk of the corporativist state; and papal interference was at an all-time low. It is not surprising that in Italy, Germany and France broad-based Christian Democratic parties emerged which emphasized democracy, human rights, Christian values, the family, and the role of small farms and small businesses. Where the political slate had been wiped entirely clean, as in Germany and Italy, the Christian Democrat parties were able to dominate the non-socialist part of the political spectrum. In France, however, the slate was quickly re-written over by the most powerful political figure to emerge from the war, General de Gaulle, who eventually engineered the political collapse of the main Christian Democrat party, the Mouvement Républicain Populaire.

The German and Italian Christian Democrats were broadly based parties with a rhetoric of Christian values of a fairly non-doctrinal kind. (In Germany the party had to appeal also to Protestants, though the majority of its voters, members and party officials has always been Catholic.) On large-scale political issues such as the degree of State control and intervention in the economy, this rhetoric could give little specific guidance. In Germany there was a political struggle within the party, during the immediate post-war years, between a left-wing element led by Jakob Kaiser in Berlin and the more moderate leadership of Konrad Adenauer. Kaiser's group demanded widespread nationalization and 'the co-determination by workers of the direction of industry'; Adenauer temporized over nationalization, agreeing it for coal but proposing an intermediate form of public ownership for iron and steel. Both Adenauer and Kaiser appealed to the same general doctrinal principles of mutual responsibility, social solidarity, and so on. In the end it was only the hard-headed realism of Ludwig Erhard which saved the party from a programme which would have been almost indistinguishable from that of the Social Democrats after 1958: Erhard insisted, in a phrase which went against the grain of most Catholic social teaching, that 'the market is the only really beneficial institution to create just and maximal distribution'.* The sheer overwhelming success of Erhard's economic and monetary policies fixed the character of the CDU's programme as essentially free-market; by way of compensation, great emphasis was put in the party's rhetoric on 'solidarity', by which was meant generous welfare provision and worker participation in the management of industry. These elements were combined in the famous catch-phrase 'soziale Marktwirtschaft', 'social market economy'. And, linked to the concept of 'social solidarity' was a special insistence on the idea of 'personality' – that is, the idea that people

* *Ibid.*, p. 139.

are to be understood and treated not just as individuals, but as 'persons', whose personhood is bound up in their membership of a community. There was a strong connection here with the thinking of Mounier, whose philosophical position was known as 'personalism'; indeed, the party programmes of some Christian Democrat parties, such as the Flemish *Christelijke Volkspartij* (Christian People's Party), specifically say that they believe in 'personalism' or 'social personalism'.

The economic success of Erhard's legacy in Germany, combined with the development of a stable two-party (or two-and-a-half-party) system, has ensured the healthy survival of the CDU. Italy, unfortunately, had no Erhard. It had an Adenauer, in the form of Alcide de Gasperi; and his party, the Democrazia Cristiana, founded in 1943, played an important part in the majority of post-war Italian governments, until its recent collapse. But the party's power-base contained a huge range of different interests and different political complexions, and the nature of the Italian political system led it into coalitions with Republicans, Liberals, Social Democrats and even, from the early 1960s to 1975, the Italian Socialist Party. (The 'historic compromise' proposed by Aldo Moro, a grand coalition of Christian Democrats and Communists, never quite came to fruition.) The early programmes of Democrazia Cristiana included some familiar themes, such as the promotion of family values and the protection of small farmers. But they also included the expropriation of large estates, new schemes for worker participation in the management of industry, and a programme of nationalization which built up a huge public sector in the Italian economy.

In the international policies of the Italian and German Christian Democrats, two common themes emerge. The first is Atlanticism: both parties were consistently in favour of Nato membership. The doctrinal substratum of this policy was of course anti-communism; but the need for some such security system was a matter of geopolitical necessity anyway. The other common theme is perhaps more revealing of the doctrinal content, such as it is, of Christian Democracy – namely, the enthusiasm of both parties for European integration. It was the leaders of the three main Christian Democrat parties, Adenauer, de Gasperi and Robert Schuman, who, together with the technocrat Jean Monnet, brought the European Community into existence. And to this day it is the Christian Democrat parties of Europe who push hardest for the creation of something resembling a common European state – as witnessed by their policy document of 1990 entitled 'Pour une constitution fédérale de l'Europe', or by the 1992 'Athens Declaration' of the European People's Party. The emphasis on federalism is closely linked to the idea of subsidiarity, which is itself drawn from Catholic social teaching. This is the doctrine that there is an ascending scale of levels of government, with each level doing those things which the levels below it cannot achieve by themselves: since, therefore, European-wide policies cannot be achieved by individual national governments, it follows that they must be carried out by a European-wide government.

Looking at the record of post-war Christian Democrat governments and parties, it is possible to find many points of overlap with British Conservatism in general and conservative realism in particular. Atlanticism is one such and, in Germany above all, respect for the essential principles of free-market economics is another. A defence of 'family values', implying a broadly conservative social policy, is another, and so too is a tendency towards a sort of cultural traditionalism, in so far as religion is bound up with the cultures of these countries. If Christian Democracy is simply a matter of what Christian Democrats do, then there are good grounds for saying that Christian Democrats are more or less Conservatives quite a lot of the time. But the nature of a political ideology is more than simply what the politicians do; it is also a matter of what they say they are doing, what they think, and even what they think they say they are doing. Some of the most distinctive features of Christian Democracy are bound up with the theories of some closely related intellectual traditions: above all, the theories of Mounier, Maritain and the papal encyclicals. Nor is it surprising that Christian Democrat politics should have been quite heavily influenced by theorists or theoretical pronouncements, since its fragmented and repeatedly interrupted history during the last hundred years or so meant that its leaders were frequently out of power, and sometimes out of politics altogether, retreating from the soapbox or the debating chamber to the library, the study, or the pew. These distinctive areas of policy include the two fields in which conservative realism and Christian Democracy are most strongly opposed: one concerns the role of the market, and the other concerns the role of the nation state. Christian Democracy is basically hostile to what it calls economic individualism; and it is ultimately inimical to the nation state. The origins of these hostilities can be understood only in the light of the theories to which they appeal.

The social teaching of the Catholic Church, as expressed in the series of modern encyclicals on these matters, was born out of a concern for the plight of poverty-stricken industrial workers. Socialism (in the strong sense of the term, meaning the mass-redistribution of wealth through expropriation and large-scale nationalization or common ownership) was always rejected; but the nature of the argument in which that rejection was expressed changed subtly between the 1890s and the 1930s. Leo XIII made it clear that he regarded socialism as a cure worse than the disease of economic liberalism. Pius XI, on the other hand, presented the two things as entirely symmetrical ills. 'Twin rocks of shipwreck', he wrote in *Quadragesimo anno*, 'must be carefully avoided. For, as one is wrecked upon, or comes close to, what is known as "individualism" by denying or minimizing the social and public character of the right of property, so by rejecting or minimizing the private and individual character of this same right, one inevitably runs into "collectivism".* This idea that there is a symmetry between economic individualism and the collectivism of expropriation and state ownership is, however, deeply misleading. As conservative realists know, a free-market economy can function well, and provide increasing prosperity for everyone, when each agent is acting in his own economic interest; it is only the malfunctioning of this so-called 'individualist' system that produces mass poverty. An economy run on a 'collectivist' principle is, on the other hand, guaranteed by its very nature to impoverish the people, whether gradually or quickly. Besides, the individualism which functions in a market is always dependent on the existence of common rules of behaviour, a community of practices and law: extreme collectivism, of the sort practised by Stalin or Mao, has to be imposed by force from above, and by its very nature destroys any such common framework. In abstract terms, the symmetry is a false one; and any political position based on the assumption that individualism and

* *Quadragesimo anno*, para. 46, in Walsh and Davies, *op. cit.*

collectivism are equal and opposite ills will in effect be unfairly hostile to the individualist side of the argument.

In concrete terms, this point may need to be made even more strongly. When judging any particular policy, it can make no sense to condemn something simply because it promotes individualism in the abstract, without referring to its concrete political circumstances. The Conservative trade union reforms of the early 1980s, for example, were often criticized by Christian Democrats on the Continent, and their sympathizers in the Conservative Party, as incitements to rampant individualism. But to condemn any move in an individualist direction as a move away from the centre is to endorse unthinkingly the status quo, even when the status quo is the damaging legacy of the socialist governments of the 1970s. Conservative realists do not make such a mistake. Besides, they know that so-called 'economic individualism' is a highly artificial theoretical construct: even when individuals are single-minded in their pursuit of wealth, they will always want to spend that wealth on their families, on shared activities, and indeed in a whole range of ways that imply communities of values.

An especially striking example of the tendency to construct false symmetries can be found in the doctrines of Emmanuel Mounier. His theory of 'personalism' claims to offer the perfect mid-point between individualism and collectivism. However, if one looks through the whole range of Mounier's writings one finds that most of his intellectual energies were spent attacking only one side of the argument – what he called 'bourgeois individualism'. The best intellectual biography of Mounier summarizes as follows: 'From the prospectus announcing the publication of *Esprit* in February 1932, to his last article in the journal, Mounier's anti-capitalism was clear.'* Capitalism, he thought, caused war, corruption, poverty, tyranny and injustice: the profit motive perverted all human values, leading to 'the bourgeois spirit'. Individualism, he argued, was the spiritual sickness from which capitalism flowed, and the origin of all human alienation. His theory of alienation was strongly influenced by Marxism, and only his reversal of the direction of causation from the spiritual to the economic prevented him from being a Marxist. One typical

* Rauch, *Politics and Belief*, p. 90.

passage in which he denounces bourgeois man will give the flavour of Mounier's style:

> On the altar of this sad world there is but one god, smiling and hideous: the Bourgeois. He has lost the true sense of being, he moves only amongst things, and things that are practical and have been denuded of their mystery ... He has deflected the universe of virtues from its supposedly senseless course towards the infinite and made it centre about a petty system of social and psychological tranquillity. For him there is only prosperity, health, common sense, balance, sweetness of life, comfort.*

The cadence of contempt in that final sentence will strike strangely on the ears of any conservative, whether realist or otherwise, for whom prosperity, health, common sense, balance, sweetness of life and comfort might indeed seem reasonable things for human beings to aim at.

The false symmetry between individualism and collectivism in modern Catholic social thought can be traced back to a more elementary failure of this body of thought to adjust to political and legal realities. When Pius XI set out his case in *Quadragesimo anno*, he put 'the social and public character of the right of property' on one side of the argument, and 'the private and individual character of this same right' on the other. But this was a fundamentally false antithesis. The 'private and individual character of the right of property' is its essential character as a legal right – that is, the legally protected area of freedom within which the property-owner can make use of his property as he wishes. The 'social and public character of the right of property', on the other hand, is a matter of moral duty or responsibility – not legal right or duty. To place these two things in exactly symmetrical relation to each other is therefore to blur the difference between law and morality. And that blurring is indeed the fundamental mistake of all Catholic social and political thought, a mistake which Leo XIII and Pius XI both warned against and then went on to commit.

* From Mounier's *Personalist Manifesto* (1938), quoted in J. Amato, *Mounier and Maritain: A French Catholic Understanding of the Modern World*, University, Alabama, 1975, p. 129.

Earlier in this paper, Leo XIII's distinction between legal duties and duties of charity was noted. He himself, nodding in the direction of Aristotle or Aquinas, described it as the difference between commutative and distributive justice. But, having said that the difference should be carefully maintained, he then went on to argue in favour of 'the just wage', and of State intervention to compensate for inequalities of wealth. Apparently his line of thought was that these were merely policy recommendations, which Catholics active in the political realm should desire to implement. It is as if he failed to see that when policy is implemented it becomes law: his argument implied that moral duties should indeed be converted into legal ones. His later successor Pius XI strengthened this tendency when he demanded that the political realm should be governed by 'social justice' (a term Leo XIII had been careful not to use). 'It is most necessary', wrote Pius XI, 'that it [social justice] be truly effective, that is, establish a juridical and social order which will, as it were, give form and shape to all economic life.'*

This was the basis of Pius XI's approval of a kind of corporativist system – just as Toniolo, in the late nineteenth century, had similarly claimed that a revival of guild corporativism would embody the scholastic principles of distributive justice. It is important to note that these proposals were not simply for new economic formations: they also implied a new kind of political structure, more removed from liberal democracy. The basic pattern of thought here is that to realize distributive justice it is not sufficient merely to produce some particular end-state; one must also have a process of achieving it in which the virtues of harmony and order are exhibited. Any simple market system, such as a labour market, is by its nature confrontational and adversarial; so too is any liberal-democratic system of political representation, in which different interests are opposed and politicians compete for votes. By trying to apply too directly to the economic and political realms a rather unitary concept of moral order, this body of Catholic teaching fails to understand that some kinds of adversarial activity may in fact be healthy things which act as the guardians of a complex system of mutual benefit. Conservative realists, who know that real politics will always be confrontational

* *Quadragesimo anno*, para. 88, in Walsh and Davies, *op. cit.*

and real economic activity will always involve a tension between supply and demand, do not make this mistake.

The doctrine on which Christian Democracy is based is a doctrine which cannot maintain any clear or workable distinction between politics and morality. To put this another way, it is a doctrine which has no real sense of the peculiar nature of the political realm. There is no place in it for a peculiarly political level of human activity: instead, following the schemes of scholastic thought on which it ultimately depends, it envisages a hierarchy – almost a continuum – of levels of human cooperation or 'community': the family, the extended family, the circle of friends, the wider social group, the local community, the regional community, the nation, the family of nations, the world. This is a theme common to Mounier's personalism, Maritain's Thomism and the teachings of the modern popes – especially Pope John XXIII, whose encyclical *Pacem in terris* (1963) includes classic statements on this subject, referring both to social order and international relations.

The concept of authority, in this scheme of things, is in a functional relation to the concept of 'the common good'. There is no *qualitative* distinction, therefore, between the authority of the chairman of a tiddlywinks society, who guards and promotes the common good of that association, and the authority of the president of a republic. This is the ultimate theoretical explanation of the enthusiasm of Christian Democrats for extending authority upwards to a new, European level. For them, there is nothing special about any particular level in this hierarchy, such as the level of national government. For a conservative (and especially for a conservative realist), the existence of a nation state, implying both the existence of a genuine political community and the exercise on behalf of that community of the kind of final political authority known as sovereignty, is not some easily adjustable contingent fact, but a crucial – rather, *the* crucial – feature of our political landscape, a landscape which centuries of history have helped to mould into its present shape.

What these considerations suggest is that, however much the policies of conservative realists and Christian Democrats may overlap in some areas, there are vital theoretical differences beneath the surface. Conservatism, viewed in the most long-term historical perspective, is not necessarily tied to liberal democracy, but present-day conservative realism values liberal-democratic institutions as the most reliable way of maintaining the health of a political community. Christian Democracy, throughout its history, have evinced a certain distaste for the confrontational and divisive nature of political action, seeking to go beyond the democratic system, either with proposals for other forms of organization (such as the corporativist one) or with appeals for moral and spiritual regeneration. Conservative realism, similarly, values the market; Christian Democracy distrusts it too, and seeks constantly to modify or moralize it. And conservative realism values the peculiar nature of a political community under a sovereign government, while Christian Democracy has no concept of sovereignty other than the theological one. Since Christian Democracy has always been anti-communist, it is possible to affirm that it has never been on the extreme left. Most major parties of the left in Western Europe today, however, are not on the extreme left either: they also appeal to personalism, solidarity and subsidiarity, as anyone who has struggled through the works of Jacques Delors or the pronouncements of Tony Blair will know. Given the range of political positions now on offer, it would not be misleading to say that Christian Democracy, in most of its basic principles and many of its practical proposals, lies today somewhere in the centre-left of the spectrum. Except that, throughout its hundred-year-old history, the trouble with Christian Democracy has been its tendency to assume that it need not be located on the political spectrum at all.

IV

THE PERILS OF PRINCIPLE

RICHARD GRIFFITHS

I will start, as all good Conservative speakers should, with a reminiscence. Just over thirty years ago, in 1964, I remember Maurice Cowling sitting with me watching a broadcast by the recently elected Prime Minister Harold Wilson. Maurice was overwhelmed: 'My God!' he said. 'The man's fantastic! He hasn't mentioned the word principle once! It's enough to tempt you to join the Labour Party!'

Maurice never did, of course, join the Labour Party; but he was to retain some amusement at the way in which that part of the liberal intelligentsia which had until then seen the Labour Party as its natural home, was repelled by what he admiringly described as the 'low tone of Wilsonian socialism'.*

There is, however, an insight to be gained from that instant reaction to Wilson's pronouncements. Harold Wilson, for all his mistaken initiatives, had a healthy scepticism as regards statements of principle which prefigured policies. Wilson never understood political activity, in Michael Oakeshott's words, as 'the activity of amending the arrangements of a society so as to make them agree with the provisions of an ideology'.** In this respect, Wilson, while most of his policies were the antithesis of Conservative, presented nevertheless, in his attitudes to political activity, something of a caricature of Conservative attitudes.

A caricature, certainly, because there are two major meanings to the word 'principle'. One is 'a fundamental assumption or proposition, forming the basis of a chain of reasoning'; the other is 'a general law

* Maurice Cowling, 'The Present Position', in *Conservative Essays*, Cassell, 1978, p. 6.

** Michael Oakeshott, 'Political Education', in *Rationalism in Politics*, Methuen, 1962, p. 125.

or rule used as a guide for action' (as in 'moral principle').* The extraordinary achievement of the Wilson governments was their apparent ability to dispense with both. What, I imagine, Maurice Cowling was praising in 1964 was not an absence of moral principle but the refreshing picture of a supposedly left-wing ideologue showing a suitable reticence with regard to ideology-ruled politics.

No one should shy away from possessing underlying principles of the second type; as Kenneth Minogue has pointed out, 'Morality is certainly something to which Conservatives ought not to be indifferent'. Nor need we dismiss the idea of fundamental propositions in politics, for (as Michael Oakeshott has pointed out), political debate may sometimes invoke schemes of abstract ideas, or general principles, which abridge political experience in order to explore its 'intimations' more closely.** But any such principles should reflect, rather than lead, political activity, and have an explicatory rather than a directive role.

As Oakeshott explains it, for a conservative, 'modification of the rules should always *reflect*, and never *impose*, a change in the activities and beliefs of those who are subject to them'. For this reason a conservative 'will be suspicious of proposals for change in excess of what the situation calls for, of rulers who demand extra-ordinary powers in order to make great changes and whose utterances are tied to generalities like "the public good" or "social justice", and of Saviours of Society who buckle on armour and seek dragons to slay.'***

It was something of an irony that, for most of his time as Leader of the Labour Party, Wilson should have been faced by a Conservative leader whose utterances were marked by generalities of this sort, and who used those generalities in order to propose change in excess of what the situation called for. Ted Heath's generalities on 'the public good', were, however, concentrated on one specific area: that of Europe. And the generalities were, in this case, almost completely unrelated to reality. Their basis was 'the European idea', a concept so vague and so all-embracing that it was clear, when one questioned it, that its proponents not only had no idea of what the 'European

* See *Oxford Shorter English Dictionary*, Clarendon Press, 1972, 'Principle'.

** Oakeshott, 'Political Education', p. 125.

*** Michael Oakeshott, 'On Being Conservative', in *Rationalism in Politics*, Methuen, 1962, p. 191.

idea' *was* or *meant*, but also had no idea of Europe itself or of its political nature. We entered Europe, therefore, on the basis of a promissory note of dubious value; and we have paid the interest on that uncertainty ever since.

The basis for our entry into Europe was therefore fundamentally flawed. Under the umbrella of the 'European idea' there were a variety of hidden agendas. The original open agenda had been economic advantage, or rather the avoidance of economic disadvantage (though even these premisses were hotly disputed, and economists were divided). This was to be an economic rather than a political union. Yet beneath the surface there already existed the political agendas which have since surfaced: political union; economic decisions (such as the entry of Mediterranean States) being governed by political criteria such as the encouragement of democracy; the gradual and apparently unstoppable erosion of national rights. And, to crown it all, the creeping spread of bureaucratic controls which far outstripped that State interference which, in the post-war period, Conservatives had associated with socialist government. Furthermore, far from the economic advantages that had been proclaimed as the potential advantages of the Community, there is clear economic disadvantage for Britain in many of the 'reforms' that are proposed by the Community.

It is, of course, possible to say that we are now faced by a new situation, in which Britain's economic base has changed, and in which to leave the European Community could be far more dangerous than it would have been not to enter in the first place. In this sense, a Conservative attitude would be to say that the onus of proof for change now lies with those who wish to remove Britain from the Market. The debate, in the present day, is as flawed as that of the early 1970s; more flawed, indeed, as in face of one lot of ideologues, the Euromaniacs, we have another, the Euro-sceptics. Each group appears to be governed by ideology rather than by a realistic assessment of the possibilities for action, and of the actual situation in which we find ourselves.

What a Conservative government should do, *as a minimum*, in the present situation, is to attempt to deal with the disadvantages of the present European system, and at the same time oppose all those initiatives which will enhance the central powers of the European

Community still further. Any change needs, as always, to be justified by a known advantage which will counterbalance the dangers of disadvantage which are fundamental to all change. European *political* union could in no way be described as advantageous change, and policies which are clearly aimed towards it, at whatever timescale, should be opposed. Monetary Union has found no justification that is convincing. Any attempt to create a common European foreign policy should, on the experience of the Balkans, for example, be strongly opposed, as should any attempt to extend the powers of the 'democratically elected' European Parliament (which is both responsible to nobody, and also irresponsible in every other sense), or any attempt to reduce the powers of the individual countries at the top level. At the same time, current abuses need to be rectified, from the Common Agricultural Policy to the inordinate red-tape and interference from Brussels. It goes without saying that the corruption which has come to light in the EC, and which has far more in common with the endemic corruption of the Latin States than with the comparatively mild home-grown variety about which the British press makes so much noise, should be rooted out.

All these things, I think, should be on the agenda of any Conservative government, and, when the fight between the ideologues subsides, will no doubt be central to the agenda of the present government.

Europe is not the only area where ideologies seem to have taken over from what Owen Harries calls 'prudent realism', however. The current Conservative Party appears, in a whole variety of areas, to have moved from decisions based on realism to those based on ideology.

It would be wrong to blame this on the Thatcher era. Despite all the rhetoric about 'freedom', despite the language equating Thatcherism with a new intellectual ideology, despite the totems and gurus, most of the decisions taken in that period were realistically based in the current situation, and grew organically out of it. As Shirley Letwin has convincingly shown in her *The Anatomy of Thatcherism*, Thatcherism had a clear identity which underpinned the decisions made in the period of Margaret Thatcher's Prime Ministership; but this identity did not depend so much on specific ideologies, as on an underlying series of *attitudes* which could be translated, if rhetorically convenient, by specific ideological stances.

Most of the policies of the Thatcher governments seem to me, despite the rhetoric, to have been based on realistic aims based on the current British position. As Shirley Letwin has put it, 'Thatcherism is to be understood not as an abstract theory but as a *practical* doctrine applying to a particular time and place.'* What were the main aims of Thatcherism in its early years? Above all, to restore, and to undo the harm that had been done to what it was proposed to restore. On the one hand, they were to conserve and restore Britain's economy, by a whole series of measures which were perceived as very unpalatable at the time. In a few years, they succeeded in placing Britain's economy once more on an even keel; despite subsequent mistakes in the latter part of the Thatcher period, which led to economic crisis, this still remains the basis for Britain's greater underlying economic strength. On the other hand, the aim was to make Britain governable once more, by taking the power from major corporative bodies like the trades unions. Linked to all this was the traditional Conservative policy of 'rolling back the frontiers of the State', coupled with an emphasis on free enterprise and competition. But, though there was a lot of political commentary attached to these policies, which appeared to make them products of a 'new ideology', they were essentially realistic Conservative responses to the situation in which Britain found itself at that time.

So, though a 'Thatcher ideology' was believed to have been created, it masked a realism and an adaptability which was led by events rather than leading them. Ideologies abridge and distort reality, by making certain conditions necessary, rather than incidental; the stuff of politics is, on the other hand, real, and far too complex to be governed effectively by any ideology. Though monetarism, for example, was extremely effective at certain stages in achieving the desired results, monetarism was a means rather than an end in itself. Policies which had appeared essential could on occasion be quietly put on the shelf. For most of her time, the then Mrs Thatcher showed exceptional sure-footedness in adapting to circumstance. The 'lady was not for turning', in the popular vision; and much of her popular appeal lay

* Shirley Robin Letwin, *The Anatomy of Thatcherism*, Fontana, 1992, p. 303.

in the image of the 'Iron Lady' who stuck firmly to her ideals against all comers. But no politician could subordinate politics to ideology, in the way that was suggested by these images, and remain a successful politician; Mrs Thatcher succeeded in quietly subverting the image that had become attached to her.

It was only in the last years of the Thatcher era that that sure-footedness deserted her, and that the Conservative government became tied to a series of unpopular and destructive policies, created in large part by individual ministers who were already showing signs of the ideological atrophy which was to characterize the administrations of her successor.

The successive mistakes of the Major administrations have been based in part on a belief that ideology governs politics. Means have become ends in themselves, and continue to be pursued even when circumstances have changed, or appear unsuitable. Privatization, for example, often seems to have become an end rather than a means. Many privatizations have been highly sensible actions which have enhanced the output and achievements of the industries concerned by introducing competition in place of monopoly, competence in place of decay, profitability in place of debt. But privatization is not in itself a virtue; there are industries for which it is less suited (the railways being a prominent example). The obsession with privatization, the trumpeting forth in the press of the 'uncompromising Conservatism' which is being exhibited by those who insist on it, are more than a pandering to those Conservatives who want to see firm stances taken; they are the signs of a fundamental weakness in governmental decision-making processes, whereby ideology has taken the place of sense, and whereby the public's reactions can be ignored, as being less important than the pursuit of a dream. The necessity, on occasion (as with the Post Office), to reverse such a policy in response to public opinion negates any public effect that such a 'firm Conservative' policy might have had. But, far from learning from this, the government seems even more determined to implement such policies; the pursuit of rail privatization, with every prospect of confusion and failure, appears to be based in a dogged determination not to back down again, rather than in an objective assessment of the situation, and of the needs of the consumer. There comes a time when governments seem to feel that the only way forward is to 'stick to their guns'. That is the time of a government's decline. We saw it with the poll tax; now we see it with a number of other central policies. The tendency is to 'stick to your guns' until too late, and then have a far more damaging climb-down. It is government by crisis.

There appears, too, to have been a serious reversal of previous Conservative attitudes with regard to the role of the State. Conservative rhetoric, for decades, has been concerned with 'rolling back the frontiers of the State', and with the freedom both of markets and of individuals. Yet the State has become ever more powerful, and its interventions in public affairs have become ever more intrusive; and 'free markets' have turned out to be, only too often, disguised monopolies which do the job worse than what preceded them.

Nowhere is the 'the State-knows-best' syndrome more evident than in the Health Service reforms of Mrs Bottomley. There is virtue in the attempt to reform, which was clearly needed; but the methods by which it has been attempted have been deplorable. Decisions, based on what are now known to be flawed presuppositions, have been made by *Diktat*, despite the paraphernalia of public consultation. They have then been communicated in a way which would have precluded democratic debate, had it not been for the vigilance of certain MPs. The justification for all this has been that a Secretary of State has to act in people's interest, even when it is against their wishes. But how does one gauge what is 'in their interest'? This particular Secretary of State's 'experts', whose names were produced in order to confute medical practitioners within the Health Service, the general public it serves, and Members of the House of Commons, turned out to be – two retired academic Heads of House, concerned above all with medical education, and now based in the House of Lords! 'The State knows best' used to be the phrase used in criticism of dictatorships. Democratic governments must take greater care to persuade the public that they *listen*, if they are not irremediably to lose the public support on which they depend. Above all, they must beware not only of listening to academics, but also of *being seen* to consider consultation with academics to be more important than consultation with those intimately concerned with a problem. The 'appeal to the expert' is always suspect, in a democratic society. Kenneth Minogue has described the 'strange, futile twitchings by which modern British society is characterized' in the following terms:

> What is immediately evident about the many changes of this kind (produced by successions of experts rather than by politicians) is that they have been imposed from above, in terms of some currently fashionable idea (economies of scale, salvation by education, rationalization and consolidation) rather than grown from below out of the vast resources of adaptability found in the lives of the people themselves. Paradoxically, the more politicians talk the language of democracy, participation and responsiveness, the more captious and dictatorial they become.*

The wide-ranging and fundamental decisions in relation to hospital closures *may* have been right in themselves (though more recent evidence as to the need for beds, etc, produced since the Tomlinson Report by, among others, Jarman, seems to point to the need for different policies); but, right or wrong, they were fundamentally *un-Conservative*, in their rejection of gradual and organic change in favour of painful root-and-branch excision; and they were *dogmatic* in a sense that is alien to Conservative thinking. It is significant that a Minister who may be taken as a standard-bearer for a return to true Conservative realism, the Secretary for State for Wales John Redwood, should have stressed, in relation to those Health Service changes for which *he* is responsible, the need for orderly and gradual change, accepting what is good in what exists, and accepting the need to think of the needs and desires of those actually served by the system.

It is interesting to note that one of the most dangerous examples of a supposedly 'free-market' system which turns out to be the opposite is also within the Health Service remit – the 'internal market' which has done so much to depersonalize health care. I spent part of last year in consultation with Health Service civil servants and with representatives of 'purchasers' and 'providers'. I came out of it all shell-shocked not just by the materialistic jargon used in relation to care for human beings, but also by the attitudes revealed by that jargon, in which the actual patients seemed to come rather far down the list. (Language in itself can be the most revealing evidence in relation to aims and presumptions.) The use of an internal market in relation to an activity which is not primarily profit-making is

* Kenneth Minogue, 'On Hyperactivism in Modern British Politics', in *Conservative Essays*, Cassell, 1978, p. 118–19.

dangerous not only because it is irrelevant, but also because it actually *causes* new problems which then have to be solved. On the large scale, it was the advent of the 'internal market' which caused the crisis in relation to the future of London's hospitals which then appeared to have to be addressed by further 'root-and-branch' action; on the small scale, the 'internal market' can lead to complications and individual misery when the market dictates the form of medical attention to be accorded or refused. Only ideology, the extension of free market practices which are successful in other areas to areas where they are completely inapposite, could produce these results.

It is significant that, at this time when the Conservative Party has become bogged down in ideology, to the extent of misjudging both political decisions and popular responses to them, at this very time the Labour Party should have come up with another Harold Wilson. Tony Blair is the same kind of successful wheeler-dealer that Wilson was – plausible, refusing to be governed by ideology, apparently presenting no threat to the status quo. The British public will no doubt wait a while before becoming as disillusioned as it eventually did with Wilson. For the moment, Blair is making the running.

Far be it from me to suggest that the Conservative Party should copy him. As I pointed out at the beginning of this paper, there are two kinds of 'principle', both of which tend to be abandoned by a pragmatic Labour Party seeking votes outside its traditional area; but longstanding Conservative attitudes represent a series of 'principles' which the Party should never abandon. These continue to be, however, principles in the sense of 'attitudes' rather than of ideological prescriptions; and one of the ways in which the Conservative Party can revivify itself is by returning to these 'attitudes' and escaping from the ideological straitjacket into which it has been tied.

The Party should look at its traditional strengths, and assess what it would mean to return to them. It is ironic that Blair, by attempting to steal the clothes of recent Conservative governments, should be risking the same disenchantment which they have received. Above all, Blair, by wooing the middle classes, is falling into the trap of making the Labour Party into a 'middle-class' party.

The Conservatives were not, traditionally, a purely middle-class party. They had a strong populist appeal, particularly within the working class. I can myself remember, from the time when I first participated in local government, the resilience of that tradition at local level, with certain working-class wards in an industrial town regularly returning Conservative councillors. Much of that has now gone, and that Council, from being one which tended to have alternating periods of Conservative and Labour rule, is now overwhelmingly Labour. One of the unfortunate by-products of the Heath era was the start of the erosion of that constituency; and, after a short period of revival at the beginning of the Thatcher era, that erosion continued, not only in the North but also in the urban South. The Conservative Party, in its serious concern to revive the national economy, has become incidentally (and, I believe, mistakenly) associated, in the public mind, with a desire for large profits for the few, with an 'upwardly-mobile' middle ground, and with lack of concern for the rest. 'Essex man' appears to have been wooed at the expense of more reliable traditional constituencies; and, as events are showing, 'Essex man' can be a fickle partner.

The Conservative Party has much to learn from the United States, which appears to possess a robust populist conservatism which is reminiscent of our Conservative past. It can learn, too, from France, that supposedly left-wing nation, heir of the French Revolution, in which the conservative right has a popular appeal across all classes.

What we need to do is move on to the ground that is being vacated by Tony Blair and his Shadow Cabinet, and appeal over their heads to their former constituency. It is not a question of abandoning principle in any way; Conservative principles, or attitudes, can and should be aimed at the majority of people in this country, and should be seen to be so. Government should become more accessible, should listen, should learn; if it is seen to do so, policies which are just, and seen to be just, can be harsh in the public interest, without forfeiting public support. Above all, government should listen to the very real concerns of people in this country, whether they involve major matters of policy, or surface matters such as those conspicuous examples of excess which have come to light as the result of governmental policies such as privatization of the utilities. This last concern, compared with major matters of policy, may seem of slight importance; but governments have to learn that public perceptions often rest on points of detail, and that to win public opinion one must take as major those concerns which have caught the public imagination, and address them. The dismissal of this issue by certain Cabinet Ministers has shown a lack of that sure-footedness which governments in any democracy need to possess.

But these are merely details; what is needed is a fundamental shift in Conservative thinking, and a strategy to capitalize on Labour's moves, by taking some of the clothes that they have discarded. Naturally the garments should be those which conform with traditional Conservative attitudes, and not those from the revolutionary traditions of the left. The Conservative Party should become once more the party of the nation and not of a class; it should be the party which reflects many of the populist beliefs which the new Labour appears to find only too painful. Chirac, in France, has shown the appeal of a conservatism that crosses all barriers. From a Thatcherite base he has moved to the populism of 'La France pour tous'.

The policies which would go to make up this new approach will need working out in detail. This is the same kind of task that the Research Department faced in the late 1940s, and which it met so successfully in relation to the circumstances of its time. Current circumstances are, of course, different, and radically different policies will be needed, to face the new Labour threat. Indeed, Conservatives need to continue to react against the 'liberal' paternalistic politics of Butskellism, as much as against the new ideologies that succeeded them. What is needed is a new populist Conservatism, based in Conservative tradition, in order to outflank the new Labour.

It is interesting to look back seventeen years, to 1978, the year in which the volume *Conservative Essays* appeared (to which both Kenneth Minogue and I contributed). One of the last messages in that volume came from George Gale, who produced a great plea for a return to populism: 'The Conservative party needs to lose its fear of the people. It needs also to stop viewing popular opinion with distaste. There is nothing the matter with populism.'*

George went on to quote with approval Maurice Cowling's statement that 'what Conservatism should mean in the seventies and the eighties, is an attempt [...] to give political form to the idea of "rolling back the frontiers of the state"'. But he gave a warning:

* George Gale, 'The Popular Communication of a Conservative Message', in *Conservative Essays*, Cassell, 1978, p. 192.

'Without recourse to popularity that attempt will be found to fail, and there will be, in consequence, no rolling back, but only an inexorable and appalling rolling forward until the state encompasses the totality of our public lives.'

And in the conclusion to the volume Maurice Cowling summed up the views expressed by the contributors as being typical of a new Conservatism that was 'less liberal and more populist' than the 'consensus Conservatism which was associated with the Conservative party in the 1950s and 1960s', and 'less liberal and more political' than 'the economic liberalism that had been associated with it since'. Echoing George Gale, he described this as a 'new Conservatism' that it was better to see as a 'traditional Conservatism brought up to date'.*

Current Conservatism has, however, abandoned populism, has eschewed traditional Conservative values, and has introduced an ideological rigidity and a State-centred decision-making process which stultify the realistic give-and-take which is essential to successful politics. If, in 1978, it was necessary for Conservatives outside Parliament to display (in Cowling's words) 'a vigilance and a suspicion which they have not normally displayed towards their leaders and representatives in Parliament', it is even more necessary now. The future of British Conservatism depends upon a violent change of tack.

* Maurice Cowling, 'Conclusion', in *Conservative Essays*, Cassell, 1978, p. 194.

V

THE FREE MARKET AND CIVIC CONSERVATISM

DAVID WILLETTS MP

1. *Whatever happened to Conservative triumphalism?*

What are the principles which define modern Conservatism? The answer has to be the free market, freedom from State control, or to be even more ambitious, simply personal freedom. Conservatives have spent most of this century fighting a socialist party committed to big interventionist, intrusive government. We fight the battle for personal freedom with energy and with relish. It is a battle which we are winning – and for several reasons.

The free market has been the most dynamic research programme in economic theory over the past 20 years. Great intellectual excitement has been generated by applying elementary economic tools (supply and demand, cost benefit analysis, the price mechanism) to areas which were wrongly thought to be somehow immune from rational economic appraisal. So privatization and internal markets within the public sector have generated a rich and ambitious policy agenda. Since 1979 our Conservative governments have moved forward like ice-breakers, ploughing their way through the frozen wastes of State control.

Technology and industrial change are also on our side, promoting individualism both in production and in consumption. For most of this century the dominant industrial model was large-scale manufacturing with hundreds of workers carrying out virtually identical tasks on long production lines. Now large firms are a declining proportion of total national output and employment. We see the rise of small firms and the breaking up of larger enterprises so that people can work in smaller groups. Rewards are increasingly not fixed on some standardized basis but individually determined (and our left-wing traditionalists, so preoccupied with explaining greater dispersion of income in terms of the tax and benefit system, completely fail to understand that the crucial explanation is greater tailoring of pay to personal skills). Technology also makes market solutions practical in areas where they were purely theoretical in the past – Alan Walters, for example, began his career as a transport economist and advocated road pricing as a way of dealing with the problems of congestion. What was then an interesting theoretical insight is now rapidly becoming a reality thanks to new technology.

At the international level, there clearly was a Manichean battle between the West and an 'evil empire'. The Soviet Union was not just a hostile power as normally understood by diplomats; it was also, as Burke called the French Revolution, an 'armed doctrine'. The collapse of the empire finally revealed the bankruptcy of the doctrine and market capitalism is now once more the model to which almost the entire world aspires.

Above all, the appeal to personal freedom has a moral authority which it is almost impossible to challenge. As Lady Thatcher so powerfully showed, people respond to the message that they are free to choose – to seize opportunities, make their own way in the world, and take responsibility for the consequences of their own actions.

The power of free market thinking, the drive of technology, the collapse of Marxism, the moral authority of the appeal to personal freedom, all mean that modern Conservatives ought to feel that the tide of ideas and events is in our favour. The main problems facing Conservatism in Britain should be triumphalism and complacency. That vigorous, exhilarating battle over the past twenty years should have left us enjoying the same domination of the political scene as Liberalism enjoyed in the middle of the last century.

On some measures that dominance is clear: seventeen continuous years in government is no mean feat. But in other ways Conservatives can still feel like an embattled minority: the media, the Church, academia are still uncomprehending and the conventional wisdom hostile. It is easy to dismiss these as the chattering classes because Conservative wisdom has its roots deep in Middle England rather than the drawing rooms of Islington. But the battle of ideas matters. It matters that Conservatives find ourselves facing what Lionel Trilling called the 'adversary culture', a culture hostile to Conservatism and much that it values. Despite all the advances we have made since 1979, the collapse of the socialist left has not given Conservatives the intellectual dominance which we deserve. We are facing a new and different line of attack; it needs to be rebutted as effectively as the old socialism of the command economy.

11. *New anxieties*

Our new critics are not the traditional Fabian socialists, those middle-class administrators with their touching faith in big government so brilliantly dissected by Shirley Letwin in *In Pursuit of Certainty*. The new critics of Conservatism are much more like the early critics of the cash nexus in nineteenth-century Britain – the great social critics such as Carlyle and Ruskin and modern critics of the 'Cultural Contradictions of Capitalism' such as Daniel Bell and Joseph Schumpeter. When Thomas Carlyle denounced what he called 'the Gospel of Mammon' 150 years ago he was setting out a line of argument which has now become the staple of the anti-conservative conventional wisdom:

> We call it a Society; and go about professing openly the most total separation, isolation. Our life is not a mutual helpfulness; but rather, cloaked under due laws-of-war, named 'fair competition' and so forth, it is a mutual hostility. We have profoundly forgotten everywhere that Cash payment is not the sole relation of human beings.*

These critics worry about the threat, as they see it, posed by rampant market forces to social cohesion and social order. This is the line of argument put forward by Sir James Goldsmith and John Gray. They dislike what they believe is the cultural disruption wrought by economic change. They sympathized with the French in their half-successful battle in the recent GATT round to keep protectionist

* Thomas Carlyle, 'Gospel of Mammonism', *Selected Writings*, Penguin, 1986, pp. 277–8.

barriers against Anglo-American culture, notably in film and television.

These arguments appeal to a strong streak of melancholy in British Conservatism, a feeling that the institutions and ways of life which we value are under threat. And the mischievous twist to the argument is to say that it is the free market, promoted by Conservative governments, which is doing the damage. We may think of ourselves as ice-breakers but they claim we are a demolition squad. That is the crucial misconception which we have to address.

It is not just a challenge from outsiders. Looking back on the passionate disputes which have dominated the Conservative Party recently, two crucial issues stand out.

The first, of course, is Europe and the future of the nation State, which is under pressure as much from the global economy and the logic of the single market as the designs of the federalists. Any Tory committed to the integrity of the United Kingdom, as we must be, recognizes that ultimately the issues involved here are far more than economic. The anxieties which the development of Europe causes Conservatives rest on the recognition that there is indeed more to Conservatism than simple economic liberalism.

The other issue which lies behind 'back-to-basics', concern about incivility and declining standards of behaviour, single parents and juvenile crime is the future of the family. The family is under pressure from changes in the labour market and ever greater mobility as well as from the explicit anti-family agenda of some. It is capitalism's hunger for talent and hatred of the waste caused by discrimination which, for example, means that more and more women are getting paid jobs. This rise in female participation in the workforce, making wives less economically dependent on their husbands, itself drives changes in the family.

There is a connection between these two issues: the nation State and the family are the two most significant non-market institutions. They have aroused such passion and confusion because Conservatives believe they cannot be reduced to the imperatives of the marketplace.

Many of the anxieties about the marketplace both from outside and within the Conservative tradition are expressed in the language of community. This reflects the idea that there is more to our relationships with our fellow citizens than exclusively market transactions. We need somehow to show in our political thought how we connect with others.

When faced with this challenge, the Conservative response over the past twenty years has been to say that a free market economy generates the resources to pay for the welfare state so we can only 'care' if we are first efficient. The trouble with this line of argument is two-fold. First, we are the party of low public expenditure and low taxes. When we are boasting about high levels of public spending on the welfare state it can sound as if those claims are being delivered through gritted teeth, like a divorcee telling his ex-wife how much alimony he is paying her. Secondly, this line of argument concedes far too much ground to our opponents. It assumes that any sort of 'solidarity' with our fellow citizens must be expressed through State activity. But in fact big government contributes to the atrophy of a far richer and more satisfying network of non-State activities. That is why Conservatives increasingly talk of the active citizen, of civil society, of community, of what the sociologists call the 'mediating structures', and Burke called the 'little platoons'. The nuances which distinguish these different terms need not detain us. What matters is that they all show an increasing recognition that it is imperative that Conservatives should not speak to the electorate exclusively in the language of economic liberalism.

There are some Conservatives who are uncomfortable with all this. Nigel Lawson briskly observes that 'Capitalism has sought to rest its case on its practical success . . . Socialism by contrast has been forced by practical failure onto the high ground of morality' (*Financial Times*. 6 September 1993). But why should we leave the devil with the best tunes? And as politics is increasingly a cultural as much as an economic battle, Conservatives need to deploy more than economic arguments.

The doubters fear that as soon as we move away from pure individualism then we will find no coherent stopping point short of old-fashioned statism. We must certainly be on our guard against that. Scratch some communitarians and underneath you will indeed find someone who wants more public spending and government intervention to stop markets doing their job. It was during the miners' strike, for example, that we heard again and again about those 'mining communities' which demanded subsidies from the rest of us so that they could survive insulated from economic change in the energy industry.

Some communitarians do demand too much of us. There was a very English correspondence in *The Times* recently amongst practising Anglicans debating on how to avoid the intrusive 'kiss of peace' which was becoming popular in the more evangelical churches. It was clear that many Anglicans preferred something more restrained and phlegmatic, perhaps a 'handshake of acquaintance'. One of the reasons Conservatives may prefer to talk of 'civility' rather than 'community' is that it reaches a rather different notch on the emotional register.

Nevertheless if we simply claim to be individualists *pur et dur* and denounce anything else as old-fashioned statism, then we will have failed to engage with the sort of issues that people now expect us to address. The communitarians are on to something and to retreat into simple-minded individualism is not true to the Conservative tradition and certainly not to the three great Conservative thinkers to whom this book is dedicated.

It would be particularly ironical as the intellectual energy behind these issues comes from new critiques of Rawls. John Rawls' *Theory of Justice*, first published in 1971, dominated political philosophy for nearly twenty years. It has now come under sustained attack from distinguished thinkers such as Alasdair MacIntyre, Michael Sandel and Charles Taylor. They criticize Rawls because, like all contractarians, he asks us to imagine being a person without being in society. This is the reason why Conservatives never fell for Rawls in the first place. He has the typical world view of the twentieth-century progressive: diversity in everything apart from income and wealth, where egalitarianism rules. Conservatives should welcome the increasing recognition of the inadequacy of that Rawlsian vision of a society where all we can do is agree to disagree and then use the government for ever more ambitious egalitarian transfers of resources.

It is absurd to imagine that any of the three thinkers we are celebrating would have settled for the simple-minded individualism which has become the media's caricature of free market Conservatism. Oakeshott had a subtle and elusive account of our identity which made him sceptical of liberal individualism with its crude ideas of what it is to be a person. Shirley Letwin, in her book, *The Gentleman* *in Trollope*, remarks that 'individuality is nothing to do with rejecting constraints or pursuing "self-realization"'. Both are ruled out because a gentleman's selfhood is made by him out of materials provided by his communal life. The richer the materials, the more subtle and various can be the product.'* This is far removed from any picture of us simply as economic agents. Elie Kedourie famously traced back the dangerous doctrine of nationalism to Kant's idea of the pure self-determining self. He preferred Hegel instead, as any true Conservative must, because Hegel understood the importance of 'what he called civil society mediating between state and individual.'**

All three of them, of course, must be counted as free marketeers; they had no truck with the idea of the State as an 'enterprise association' trying to steer economic activity. But at the same time they celebrated the ties of affinity and loyalty which are very different from the perfectly mobile, frictionless, atomistic individuals of free market theory.

These sorts of issues generate new perplexities for Conservatives. That battle with statist socialism worked on the Conservative Party like a magnet, neatly giving order to a pile of iron filings. We knew we favoured the individual against the State – and that must remain true. But the rise of new social and cultural issues obliges us to think more deeply about our Conservatism. The trouble is that the 'adversary culture' identified by Lionel Trilling, or what the Americans now call the 'counter-culture', has generated a corrupted version of the individualism which is at the heart of the British political tradition. It has degenerated into self-gratification without constraint. When Neil Kinnock in his famous speech denounced the culture of 'me', 'here', 'now', he thought he was denouncing the market economy. But the market economy is capable of the most ambitious long-term projects such as the billions invested in the North Sea before a barrel of oil came onshore. Moreover it rests on a view of individuals in which they have self-control, long-term purposes, a desire to better themselves, etc. The market economy was the wrong target for him to tilt at. The real source of those attitudes which he was attacking

* Shirley Letwin, *The Gentleman in Trollope: Individuality and Moral Conduct*, Macmillan, 1982, p. 64.
** Elie Kedourie, *Nationalism*, Blackwell, 1993, p. 29.

was the moral nihilism, the relativism, the 'anything goes' attitude which we can trace back above all to the 1960s.

One reason (although certainly not the only one) why Conservatives cannot ignore all this, even if we wanted to stick to our tried and trusted economic arguments, is that these cultural changes have an economic impact. One thing we know about family breakdown, for example, is that it costs a lot of money and taxpayers end up having to help single parents with the cost of raising their children. Vandalism and crime impose high costs, particularly in our inner cities, and drive businesses elsewhere. Even such narrow economic arguments show the significance of these social changes.

A few years ago it was fashionable for Conservatives to say that they were 'dry in economic policy but wet on social issues'. It became such a cliché that one was almost desperate to find a brave soul who would claim to be wet in economics but dry in social policy – perhaps a believer in prices and incomes policies enforced by corporal punishment. But what we are now discovering is that a tough approach to fiscal policy rests on crucial assumptions about self-control, prudence, indeed behaviour generally. These are the issues which economics solves by assumptions about economic agents but which politicians cannot assume away. Ultimately fiscal Conservatism depends on the character of the people.

The economic arguments for the free market are not only right, they are also familiar to us. We jobbing politicians are by and large able to explain why we need low inflation, why financial laxity has been the bane of economic management in this country since the war, why we want low taxes. It is much more tricky to find the right words to express the significance of the increase in the number of single parents, to strike the right balance between professional ethos and external audit in maintaining standards, or to address demands to ban video nasties.

These are deep waters. Let us pause for an anecdote told by Lord Longford about a conversation he had with Stanley Baldwin. It neatly conveys the Conservative sense that something important is happening here and some uncertainty about exactly what it is.

> One Sunday afternoon, a guest of Lord and Lady Salisbury at Hatfield, I was told that Mr Baldwin wished me to go for a walk

> with him. I was flattered but surprised. He was not supposed to feel at ease with the young or with intellectuals of any age . . . As we made our way across the countryside the conversation lagged painfully. Only once, when I mentioned his son Oliver (at that time a Labour MP and supposed to have caused his family a lot of anxiety) did Mr Baldwin brighten. 'Dear fellow,' he exclaimed, coming to life suddenly. Then we trudged on again in virtual silence. Finally, as the house came in sight, I grew desperate. Somehow I must find out a little of the profound political philosophy with which I unquestioningly credited my leader. I informed him that I was teaching political theory for the Workers' Educational Association in the Potteries, and asked him which were the political thinkers to whom he himself owed most. He reflected for a moment and then spoke quietly and emphatically: 'There is one political thinker who has had more influence than all others – Sir Henry Maine. When I was at Cambridge, his authority was complete and I never ceased to be grateful for all I learnt from him.'
>
> I was, of course, all ears. After all, the walk had been anything but in vain. 'What,' I persisted, 'would you say was Maine's supreme contribution?' Mr Baldwin paused perhaps a shade longer and then said with conviction, 'Rousseau argued that all human progress was from contract to status. But Maine made it clear once and for all that the real movement was from status to contract.' He paused again, and this time for quite a while, and suddenly a look of dawning horror – but at the same time of immense humanity and confederacy – stole across his face. 'Or was it,' he said, leaning just a little towards me, 'or was it the other way round?'*

The irony of this story is that the shift from status to contract is indeed crucial to what we are talking about.

* Earl of Longford, *Eleven at Number Ten*, quoted in the *Oxford Book of Political Anecdotes*, ed. Paul Johnson, Oxford University Press, 1989.

III. *Civic Conservatism*

The task is to define the authentic Conservative position which escapes the perils of the progressive liberals, of the over-demanding communitarian and of the aggressively individualistic neo-liberals. The thought of Oakeshott, Kedourie and Letwin offers us a way forward. The starting point has to be the *institutions* which shape us and give life its meaning (hence what I have called 'Civic Conservatism').*

It is the difference between Kant, whom Kedourie attacked, and Hegel, whom he praised. Duties do not come from contracts which are voluntarily entered into but are inescapable parts of our life history as members of a community. This was why Hegel rejected Kant's notion of morality as the decisions of autonomous moral agents which are rational in the sense of being universally applicable. He understood that many moral obligations are not abstract and universal (Moralität), but are embodied in particular social relations (Sittlichkeit). There are duties such as to our children, to our neighbours, and even more specific ones such as participating in the legal system through jury service. They could not be expressed or understood outside a particular set of institutions or a culture. These are duties which only make sense because of particular social institutions which already exist. We are, if you like, born into them. The institutions which have shaped our lives in this country – the nation State, the family, private property – are the real source of our obligations to others, much deeper than some notional contract between shadowy, cultureless individuals.

Institutions tie us down with particular sets of obligations. They shape our behaviour and make us rub along with our fellows. This understanding of the important institutions can help rescue communitarianism from a dangerously woolly interventionism. On its own, communitarianism is rather invertebrate and shapeless. A community means nothing unless it is embodied in a particular set of institutions which enable people to work effectively for shared purposes. One of the most revealing episodes in recent British social policy was, for example, the shift in policy on care for the mentally

* David Willetts, *Civic Conservatism*, Social Market Foundation, 1994.

handicapped and the mentally ill. We were told that they were all suffering in something horrible called 'institutions' and instead they should thrive in what was called the 'community'. There were certainly some appalling examples of Victorian Gothic piles in which the mentally handicapped or disturbed had been immured for decades. But a community is nothing without an elaborate institutional framework. Now, slowly, we are rediscovering the need for highly-structured and sophisticated arrangements to help those discharged from the old-fashioned long-stay institutions. The sensible policy is to replace those old institutions with new, more local, more flexible institutional arrangements, not to abandon institutions altogether. The belief that somehow institutions and communities were diametrically opposed was a most revealing intellectual error.

Such a Tory reliance on institutions may seem tame, insufficiently ideologically strenuous to an outsider. But this is to fail to understand our political culture. We are after all a nation where the ultimate sign of social distinction is to be wearing an old suit which belonged to one's father. A long and continuous history has given us some confidence in time as a sort of evolutionary test of the quality and value of the institutions which we have inherited. Perhaps this is the touchstone of the Conservative realism of Oakeshott, Letwin and Kedourie. It is captured in the following famous quotation from Burke's *Reflections*:

> We are afraid to put men to live and trade each on his own private stock of reason; because we suspect that this stock in each man is small, and the individuals would do better to avail themselves of the general bank and capital of nations, and of ages. Many of our men of speculation, instead of exploding general prejudices, employ their sagacity to discover the latent wisdom which prevails in them. If they find what they seek, and they seldom fail, they think it more wise to continue the prejudice, with the reason involved, than to cast away the coat of prejudice, and to leave nothing but the naked reason because prejudice, with its reason, has a motive to give action to that reason, and an affection which will give it permanence.'*

* Edmund Burke, *Reflections on the Revolution in France*, Penguin, 1986, p. 183.

Michael Oakeshott, Shirley Letwin and Elie Kedourie are precisely such 'men' (and women) of speculation praised by Burke.

Can these insights gain some further theoretical underpinning? Sadly Oakeshott's epistemology eludes most of us. Perhaps modern game theory can help. Robert Axelrod's important book, *The Evolution of Co-operation*, has studied rigorously the so-called prisoner's dilemma. This is the dilemma in which you get off lightly if you betray your friend; you are punished severely if he betrays you and the best strategy is for neither prisoner to betray the other. If they cannot rely on each other they may well end up betraying each other. The question is in what circumstances the cooperative strategy of non-betrayal will emerge. Axelrod shows that if the prisoner's dilemma is not a one-off but encountered again and again, then the best strategy is tit for tat. If you are betrayed you betray as well, if you are not betrayed, you do not betray in return. Provided that people know they will carry on playing the game in the future, they start with non-betrayal. This may all sound rather esoteric, but it has great practical significance because institutions create environments in which we know that we will carry on dealing with people in the future.

These transactions need not even be face to face dealings with known individuals. It just has to be a framework in which we know that we will experience similar decisions again and again. Take the hurly-burly of London traffic. Sitting in the back of a taxi one is struck by how polite and considerate taxi drivers are to each other (as against what can be rather different behaviour towards the rest of us). They have a code of mutual assistance which does not depend on their knowing exactly who is driving another cab, but it is a strong social institution which they all have an overall interest in preserving.

One of the more bizarre experiments in social science is dropping wallets in the street with a sum of money and an address. The rate at which wallets are returned is a good measure of social morality. One of the findings is that when there are documents in the wallet suggesting that the owner is foreign, the wallet is less likely to be returned. The person involved is not thought to be quite sharing in the same social network.

The next question is which environments are most likely to be conducive to the creation of these sorts of social conventions and institutions whereby we act to each other's benefit without external coercion. All the evidence is that these arrangements flourish in conditions where government is limited and the free market reigns.

Book Three of Hume's *Treatise of Human Nature* is the greatest attempt in British political thought to grapple with the question of how these arrangements emerge. Hume traces them to the slow discovery of enlightened self-interest:

> I observe, that it will be for my interest to leave another in the possession of his goods, provided he will act in the same manner with regard to me. He is sensible of a like interest in the regulation of his conduct. When this common sense of interest is naturally express'd, and is known to both, it produces a suitable resolution and behaviour. And this may properly enough be call'd a convention or agreement betwixt us, tho' without the interposition of a promise; since the actions of each of us have a reference to those of the other, and are perform'd upon the supposition, that something is to be perform'd on the other part. Two men, who pull the oars of a boat, do it by an agreement or convention, tho' they have never given promises to each other. Nor is the rule concerning the stability of possession the less deriv'd from human conventions, that it arises gradually, and acquires force by a slow progression, and by our repeated experience of the inconveniences of transgressing it. On the contrary, this experience assures us still more, that the sense of interest has become common to all our fellows, and gives us a confidence of the future regularity of their conduct: And 'tis only on the expectation of this, that our moderation and abstinence are founded.*

A good recent account of the emergence of this behaviour in practice is Hernando de Soto's book, *The Other Path*. He shows how in Peru monstrous Kafkaesque burdens of regulation and taxation have driven most economic enterprise into the black economy. They are, if you like, in a state of nature with none of the usual legal protection. But this is not an atomistic anarchy. Far from it, instead the 'illegals' or

* David Hume, *A Treatise of Human Nature*, ed. L. A. Selby Bigge, Oxford: Clarendon Press, 1978, p. 490.

'informals' have developed their own conventions which indeed soon become institutions. For example, he describes how they take over land: 'First, the informals occupy the land, then they build on it, next they install infrastructures, and only at the end do they acquire ownership.'*

Of the 331 markets in Lima, 274 have been built by black-marketeers. Ninety-five per cent of public transportation belongs to them as the black-marketeers have invested more than a billion dollars in vehicle maintenance. Half the population of Lima lives in houses built by black-marketeers. Between 1960 and 1984 the State constructed low-income housing at a cost of $173.6 million but in the same period, the housing built by the black-marketeers was valued at over $8 billion. This betokens not just great entrepreneurial energy but the ability to create genuinely functioning institutions in a parallel sector completely outside the State and the legal system.

Our own experience this century has shown how the real threat to these institutional arrangements comes not from the free market but from big government. The nineteenth century saw economic and social change just as profound as today. Government was limited, but at the same time the Victorians were extraordinarily successful in 'remoralizing' the poor, as Gertrude Himmelfarb has shown. Rates of crime, drunkenness and illegitimacy, all declined. It is this century which has seen big government elbowing aside working-class self-help and private provision and weakened the institutions which shaped our characters.

The point is neatly conveyed by the anecdote of James Baker when he was the American Secretary of State visiting Romania after the collapse of Ceaucescu's regime. He was being briefed by the Romanians about the problems they had with the large number of orphans in their country. He observed that with such limited public resources they would presumably need volunteers to help care for the children. His Romanian interpreter paused. He did not recognize the word 'volunteer'. Eventually he turned to James Baker and said: 'Do you mean nuns?' It was an American Republican from Texas who had an understanding of voluntary associations which had been lost after fifty years of command socialism.

* Hernando de Soto, *The Other Path*, Taurus, 1989, p. 17.

IV. *Realism about markets*

Now we can come back to our starting point – the Conservative commitment to the free market. But instead of a piece of economic theory isolated in a political and cultural vacuum we can now see a market economy as a complex social institution. Instead of being theoretical about the free market, we can now appreciate it in that spirit of Conservative realism which imbues this book.

As for those radical individualists, Conservatives can look them in the eye and assure them that we are free marketeers, but have reached a fuller understanding of the free market through a different process of development. We begin with private property. It is significant that attempts at market reform in the countries of the Eastern bloc have failed when they have not understood that legitimate private property is the starting point for economic endeavour. If cash has no legitimacy and nobody owns anything it is very difficult for a free market to operate successfully. One of the silliest criticisms of economic policy since 1979 has been from those (some claiming to be free marketeers) who claim that we could have achieved the same progress in improving the performance of the old nationalized industries by opening them up to greater competition without privatization. The so-called free marketeers who have argued this proposition have completely failed to understand the importance of ownership in a free market.

But Conservatives understand more than simply private property: a network of institutions and indeed a culture underpins a modern successful free market economy. Just as an individual is embedded in a culture, so is a market. Visiting Hong Kong recently, it was depressing how some of the Chinese businessmen there simply did not understand why Hong Kong was an economic success. They thought that their commercial dynamism would ensure that whatever the political and constitutional regime, Hong Kong would inevitably carry on thriving. There are similar exaggerated hopes of an economic transformation of China. But these simple-minded optimists were brought up short when McDonald's, having taken a 20-year lease for a prime site in Peking, found themselves after two years unilaterally deprived of the site by order of Peking Council. Suddenly the importance of private property, and contracts enforced by an independent judiciary, becomes clear, and those abstract discussions of promise-keeping and contracts in the great writers of the Scottish Enlightenment come to life.

By contrast, our own history is one in which property and the free market are deeply embedded. The historical truth is not just that Britain is a free market society but that it was the first market society. The most recent history of London observes that 'trade came first: unlike many European cities, London's raison d'être was a market not a fortress'.* Alan Macfarlane's classic study, *The Origins of English Individualism* (Blackwell 1978), offers a fascinating account of England before the Industrial Revolution. He shows that, unlike the Continent, England never experienced the classic medieval social order: there were no English peasants in the traditional sense. Free men were selling their labour and exchanging land all through the Middle Ages.

We now know from a careful study of the village of Holywell cum Needleworth in the Prime Minister's own constituency of Huntington that of 140 families studied, fifty-one failed to maintain residence for longer than a generation. And when was this high rate of mobility? Between 1250 and 1450. In this way, Macfarlane painstakingly assembles the evidence which shows 'that the majority of ordinary people in Britain from at least the thirteenth century were rampant individuals, highly mobile both geographically and socially, economically "rational", market-oriented and acquisitive, ego-centred in kinship and social life'.**

To believe that Britain underwent the Industrial Revolution and then became a free market economy is to misunderstand the historical process. Britain was the first free market society and was thus ripe for the Industrial Revolution.

One piece of evidence in support of this interpretation, which is directly relevant to today's policy arguments about the environment, is the network of property rights in the countryside. American environmentalists have now recognized that one of their biggest problems is that much of the Mid West belongs to the Federal Government and does not have enlightened owners concerned to maintain the value of their property. They look with envy at the

* Roy Porter, *London: A Social History*, Hamish Hamilton, 1994, p. 12.
** Macfarlane, *The Origins of English Individualism*, p. 163.

intricate network of property rights established in England by the end of the Middle Ages – fishing rights, hunting rights, laws of trespass, laws about the use of common land. The 'natural' beauty of the English countryside is a testament to the centuries of inherited property rights. By contrast, as Alice Coleman has shown, the desolation and alienation of the inner city estate is a direct consequence of the lack of clear property rights.

There are deep and intricate links between markets and culture which Conservatives need to understand, treasure, and celebrate. It helps to cast doubt on, for example, the latest piece of conventional wisdom that globalization is going to lead to a massive shift of jobs and economic activity to the Third World. This rests on the belief that manufacturing moves around like water slapping about in a swinging bucket. First it all rushed to Korea and Hong Kong. Now it is all going to rush to China or the old Eastern bloc. But this is to misunderstand economic mobility and the links between commerce and culture. We are slowly discovering how much enterprise is culturally specific. Some basic manufacturing processes may now require a human input so standardized and universal as to be able simply to move to the lowest cost producer. But it is wrong to think that all economic activity is like this. Economic mobility is really the process whereby firms discover the comparative advantage of different locations.

Professor Michael Porter's interesting work on the clustering of industries shows how, instead of restlessly shifting around the world, industries instead congregate in specific locations. Why are so many of the world's motor-racing cars engineered and repaired within fifty miles of Oxford? Why is any boat in the world likely to contain some equipment made within fifty miles of my coastal constituency of Havant? The latest slogan for managers is 'think globally, act locally' – and it is a very good Tory slogan too.

v. *Conclusion*

One of the strengths of British Conservatism is a talent for forward-looking memory. We start with our history from which we can discover our national identity. We are traders and developers, entrepreneurs and speculators, free-booters and buccaneers. London's clubs and coffee houses turned into what was the world's insurance market: so much for the belief that there is some new and dangerous process by which markets subvert ancient social institutions. A recent history of eighteenth-century England draws its title from Blackstone's description of us as a 'polite and commercial people': it is not a bad picture to have of ourselves. That historical vision then guides us into the future as enterprising, flexible, vigorous free marketeers.

De Gaulle was supposed to have 'une certaine idée de la France'. We Conservatives have a certain picture of Great Britain. Enterprise and commerce are at the heart of it and so is something else: recognition that we are endowed as richly with institutions as any country in the world. Those institutions have emerged over centuries of limited government and have been threatened this century, as never before, by the rise of big government. They shape our behaviour and give our country its stability. It is why Conservative patriotism is not quite the same as the blood and soil nationalism of the Continental variety. We love our country because we love its institutions and the way of life they sustain.

Conservatives are the party of economic dynamism and institutional, particularly constitutional stability. Labour get it the wrong way round. They still have an itch to intervene to stop the processes of economic change whilst at the same time they embrace every fad that would undermine our institutions and ways of governing ourselves. They are the party of economic stagnation and restless constitutional innovation. We welcome the dynamism of the free market but understand that at the same time, people want to keep the settled institutions of this country which provide a focus for loyalty and stability in a changing world.

Economic dynamism and constitutional stability is an authentic Conservative message and one to which I believe the electorate responds.

VI

CONSERVATIVE REALISM: THE DISPOSITION OF SCEPTICAL FAITH

TIMOTHY FULLER

In discussing conservative realism as sceptical faith, I propose to focus on the conservative disposition. I do so not because it is impossible to outline a system of principles that might describe something called conservatism, but because the most distinguished exemplars of conservative realism such as, for example, Elie Kedourie, Shirley Letwin and Michael Oakeshott, reminded us to be suspicious of all 'isms'. Though there was seldom any doubt about where they stood on the issues of the day, they were consistent on this point in their thinking and in the conduct of their lives. They thought that systematization offered only the illusion that one knew more than one could ever know. Like Montaigne, they thought that the expansiveness and variability of experience would always outstrip every effort to manage and control them through the imposition of categories.

As I understand it, the conservative realist adheres to the ancient tradition of common sense and resists abstract concepts. The conservative realist does not begin with a theory about life in order to 'apply' it to the world of goings on, but begins from the life actually lived and chastens all abstract conclusions by frequent reference back to the experiential ground which prompted such conclusions. There must be a dialectic between conduct and reflection.

The conservative realist is attracted by, but sceptical about, human aspirations and claims to wisdom, especially about policies that speak in universal terms, forgetting the local circumstances in which we will experience such policies. The conservative realist expects there will always be folly and sin, doubts the permanency of both triumphs and defeats, finding little evidence that human achievements are cumulative.

Nevertheless, the conservative realist recognizes the necessities of practical life and the need for action. The conservative realist does not require utopian hopes to find motivation, believing that the modern faith in abstract ideals need not be the means to energize us. Being realistic, however, the conservative realist will employ, to the point necessary, the rhetorical style of the day, acknowledging the irony that is familiar enough from a sceptic's point of view. Above all, though, the conservative realist, even in the heat of action, hopes to perform the recollective function of acknowledging the limits to the power of human beings to transform themselves and their world into a flawless condition.

The conservative disposition which conveys this sense of the realities of life, shows itself in the capacity to see directly what is before it but also what is permanently present in the midst of the particularities of our historical situation. There is, for one of conservative disposition, the experience of transcendence in the midst of our temporal, crumbling dust, accompanied by the acceptance that we cannot liberate ourselves from our mortal condition even in encountering eternity in the midst of time. That is why we cannot reduce the conservative disposition to specific policies or programs even though in politics we must, of course, respond to current conditions, and we must risk distancing ourselves from the transcendent in attending to the daily demands of life.

One might think that our world, so preoccupied with change and innovation as it is, would be especially attuned to our temporal, mortal condition. The opposite seems to be the case. Rather, the current preoccupation – one might say obsession – with change suggests flight from admission of the basic facts of the human condition, as the conservative realist understands them, in a quest for a failsafe reality. This quest depends on the hope that ours is a temporarily distorted state of affairs to be set right by continual alteration until it assumes its putatively undistorted perfection.

In a world thus preoccupied with change, those of conservative disposition are accused of being defensive by those 'devoted to change'; they are, it is alleged, unwilling or unable to adjust to changing times, incapable of generating enthusiasm for reconstructing the order of the day. In defending something, however, the conservative realist is not negatively defensive, but constructively steadfast. This disposition is often described as traditionalist, an appropriate term for one of this sceptical disposition, provided the connection is spelled out.

It is, perhaps, a thankless task to swim against the rhetorical tide by ascribing intelligibility to tradition, but some attempt to evoke its meaning is necessary. People with a respect for tradition experience change as loss no less than gain, and they are often more eloquent in lament than in celebration. But they are no less able to cope with change. They know as well as anyone that

> We cannot revive old factions
> We cannot restore old policies
> Or follow an antique drum

But because respecters of tradition also know that change means loss as well as gain, they resist both revolutionary moralism and the pettier demands that 'doing something' is always better than not doing something. They do not neglect to recall what is permanently true of the human condition. In recalling and reminding us, their design is not to produce an uplifting experience; conservative realists are often cheerful none the less, even when soberly insisting on contingency and limits. This is mistaken frequently for nostalgia or a design for going back to what is past. It may excite the accusation of irrelevance as if the issue were solely one of this or that policy. But it is not alone, or even principally, a question of policy. What is recalled to mind by those of conservative disposition is what persists into and through the present, apprehended in the struggle of those who see what there is to see against the siren calls of forgetfulness arrayed against them. This is not a slavish insistence on a fixed, unalterable vocabulary. The continual renewal of expression is a central element of the response to the pressures of ever altering conditions. The encounter of the persistent with the momentary, of the 'what has been' with the 'what is to come,' is unending.

The conservative disposition is thus, in the first instance, philosophically and poetically, rather than politically engaged. Philosophy and poetry manifest the limits to the claims of comprehensiveness emergent in the pretensions of politics. They do so not by contesting politics for power. This disposition is mistaken for antiquarian obsession when it is really a profound critique of rationalist re-engineering. One of this disposition is not moved to go back to some imagined superior past moment but is moved rather to catch sight of what is in the interstices of what presently disguises it, to enjoy to the full the resources presently available.

Those of conservative disposition find this recollective engagement inescapable. It can be resisted but it cannot be eradicated. Invoking past experience is only metaphorically going back. When, for example, we invoke the great books of our civilization, we are not going back to an earlier time, we are making vivid to ourselves the presentness of thought about, and response to, the human condition, eliciting our own thought and response. The works we call great evoke dialogue, both provoking and constraining our subjectivity, rescuing us from easy opinions, imposing upon us the hard distinction between opinion and knowledge, between advocacy and the search for understanding.

Tradition is the continuation of dialogue through time. It is what prevents us from obliterating the presence of past thought upon the human predicament. Tradition – participation is an inherited way of thinking and talking that yet undergoes constant alteration – cannot rescue us from change; it will assist us in keeping our balance as we navigate through inevitable alteration. To invoke tradition is not to abandon the drama of life, but to find significance in dialectical engagement between the inescapable polarities of past and present that constitute our conscious existence. From this perspective, the lust for novelty is overrated, stemming from the fear of having nothing to say, and from believing that to speak of what has always been true is the misfortune of irrelevance.

The philosophical point of the conservative realist, manifested in the conservative disposition, is that it is not actually possible to dispense with connections to the past.

We can understand them superficially and attempt to deny them; we can regret what we understand our past to be, but we cannot live as if it never was. We may be moved to resistance or affirmation, but neither resistance alone nor affirmation alone could fully disclose what it is to be human. We must suffer through periods of uncertainty and disagreement – as we do today – about how to understand ourselves. In all circumstances those of conservative disposition will seek to respond conversationally instead of argumentatively. In itself, this shows that those of this disposition engage politically in light of something else prior and superior to politics. As Michael Oakeshott put it,

> In a conversation the participants are not engaged in an inquiry or a debate . . . Thoughts of different species take wing and play round one another, responding to each other's movements and provoking one another to fresh exertions . . . There is no symposiarch or arbiter . . . Conversation . . . is an unrehearsed intellectual adventure . . . it is impossible in the absence of a diversity of voices: in it different universes of discourse meet, acknowledge each other and enjoy an oblique relationship which neither requires nor forecasts their being assimilated to one another.*

One notes here the acceptance of diversity as natural coupled with the absence of the anxiety to attain perfection or uniformity.

Conversation, like law, is not a convenient instrument of policy and activists undergo a sense of deprivation when conversation, resisting debate, ignores their felt need to reach conclusions which, nevertheless, they understand as instigations.

Politics displaces conversation with debate and lives by victories and defeats. Politics is hard pressed to see that its driving force is the continual pursuit of 'ought-to-be's' that are not yet come to pass. The hope of perfection is at war with reliance on perpetual enjoyment of unfinished business. This incoherency may be seen as the charm and attraction of politics. Yet politics is also liable to be indifferent to its own self-delusions or to define its success by transitory achievements, appearing in sharp relief for what it is only against the emotional and intellectual integrity of the poet and the philosopher. This no doubt encouraged Plato's speculations on the reconciliation of philosophy and politics in a philosopher-king, but led him finally to acknowledge, and to dramatize in Socrates, the tragic opposition of philosophy and politics when efforts are made to make them more than sweet enemies.

* 'The Voice of Poetry in the Conversation of Mankind' in Michael Oakeshott, *Rationalism in Politics and Other Essays*, ed. Timothy Fuller, Liberty Press: Indianapolis, 1991, pp. 489–90.

From the perspective of the conversationalist, debate over policy is a regrettable, if unavoidable, flight from the comprehensive character of human experience, demanding that a part stand in for the whole.

Lacking anxious longing for perfection, conversation acknowledges novelty's intrusion without overrating it. Of course, every moment is new and is the harbinger of the unanticipated. Yet it is also the occasion for relearning in new terms what we have already learned. Aristotle saw long ago that conflict between equality and merit in debates over justice would be interminable since the claims on one side cannot be perfectly reconciled with those on the other side. This is no less true for us than for Aristotle despite the prodigious efforts of numerous contemporary moral philosophers to formulate plans to distribute everything fairly once and for all. One need not think of Aristotle as a conservative realist to see the connection.

A pronounced modern tendency – not tied to any specific ideological program, but implicit in all of them – lusts for change, is bored with conversation, prefers activism over reflection, fears the past, demands diversity as a function of seeking homogeneity, believes in an ideal pattern of existence distorted and disguised by actual current arrangements.

For the conservative realist there is no ideal pattern to distort. All our aspirations must emerge as possibilities from the prevailing conditions which will necessarily shape our conception of where to go from here. Since this age little respects merely habitual, unselfconscious conduct, one might expect greater reflection on what is outside our own particularity, but one expects in vain. It seems a humiliating comedown for many today to admit that

> There is only the fight to recover what has been lost
> And found and lost again and again: and now, under conditions
> That seem unpropitious. But perhaps neither gain nor loss.
> For us there is only the trying. The rest is not our business.

The conservative disposition, then, reveals a particular dialectical combination of scepticism and faith, emanating from the classical tradition of political and religious thought, which modern thought turns on its head. In an unpublished manuscript of the 1950s, Michael Oakeshott explored the politics of faith and the politics of scepticism as these appear in the modern world, and, in doing this as he did it, he exemplified the conservative disposition. He showed that there is a distinctively modern kind of immanentist faith which is a kind of faithlessness compared to ancient scepticism which could be a ground of faith in the earlier sense.

To understand this modern faithlessness, let us contrast to it Saint Augustine. Augustine's scepticism towards the world emanated from a faith, engendered in encounter with the divine, which demanded scepticism about dependence on worldly success and historical achievement. Faith in worldly monuments, no matter how grand, was actually faithlessness. The modern way inverts this: We are expected to be sceptical both about engagements which do not yield visible, material results, and about studies which formulate no policies and do not enhance techniques of social engineering.

The scepticism of Socrates or Saint Augustine towards worldliness stems from the awareness that honest self-examination compels us to confess intellectual arrogance, pretence and sin. To discover flaws in others is a self-reflection on our own capacity to be tempted by the same and to recognize temptation in others because we find it in ourselves. Or as Hobbes put it, we have to learn to see what is true not of this or that man, but of all men, including ourselves.

Oakeshott's philosophizing was constituted out of a combination of Socratic dialectic, Montaigne's perception of the inadequacy of propositions and categories to subdue and manage the totality of experience, and Hegel's method of grasping the field of political action by identifying the polarity of opposed ideals that animate the field of action in any historical period. These resources were leavened by Augustine's anti-Pelagian depreciation of politics and worldly achievement, which informed Oakeshott's thinking throughout his life.

In the soon to be published *The Politics of Faith and the Politics of Scepticism* (*PFPS*), written in the early 1950s, Oakeshott was at his most Hegelian, characterizing the last five centuries in European politics as exhibiting an ambiguous political vocabulary formed as a response to the felt need to honour two master ideals, neither of which has vanquished the other and which have not been reconciled, and each of which displays a distinctive political style. Oakeshott's own scepticism, and his qualified preference for the politics of scepticism over the politics of faith, follow from his deciding that neither ideal has comprehended the whole truth; thus the assertion of the one incites the counter-assertion of the other in an interminable tension which is the ground of what we think and do. What is true for us cannot be rendered once and for all in simple propositions, but can only be sought in pursuing intimations in a complex field of action constituted by the unresolved oppositions of our era. The truth that eludes us thus cannot be found in rationalist statements, in ideological programs or plans.

Oakeshott's philosophical scepticism requires him to be sceptical of the abstract ideal 'politics of scepticism' as well as the abstract ideal 'politics of faith'. In a sort of Socratic *aporia*, Oakeshott concluded we still do not know what we need to know in order to advance beyond the ambiguous legacy of political thought we have inherited.

By the 'politics of faith' Oakeshott did not mean the politics informed by traditional religious belief. Rather, he meant governing in the service of the perfection of mankind, in opposition to traditional religious belief, especially Augustinian. In this usage, the politics of faith actually pointed to what, from the ancient perspective, is faithlessness. The politics of faith rests on certain assumptions, uncritically accepted.

First,

> In the politics of faith, human perfection is sought precisely because it is not present . . . [but] we need not, and should not, depend upon the working of divine providence for the salvation of mankind . . . confidence in the evanescence of imperfection springs here from faith in human power and not from trust in divine providence. (*PFPS*)

Second,

> Man is redeemable in history because he is a creature of circumstances and is alterable as a consequence of altering circumstances.

Third,

> The chief agent of improvement that culminates in perfection is government. The politics of faith seeks human perfection

> through the activity of governing as the control and organization of human activity.

According to Oakeshott, 'the prime condition of the emergence of the politics of faith' was 'a remarkable and intoxicating increase of human power' which began to occur at the beginning of modern history, and which became associated not only with virtue or salvation but also with prosperity, abundance, welfare. 'We must be clear,' says Oakeshott, 'that what we are considering is an understanding of the activity of governing which attributes to ourselves the impossibility of being human without loving gain.' (*PFPS*)

To Socratics and Augustinians, the world is full of uncertainty and complex mystery that will not fully disclose themselves. It is a world in which our power is always insufficient, and we are in need of grace; a world where, maddeningly, the wicked prosper and the innocent suffer. The choice, then, can only be between alternative responses to our temporality and mortality. In the tension between the temporal and the eternal, humanity becomes conscious of itself. The very denial of this tension cannot but reveal its implicit pressure upon us.

Oakeshott acknowledges that many proponents of what he terms the politics of faith will reject the perfectionist or millennialist tag. He distinguishes 'obtrusive millennarians' from the 'improvers who deny utopian pretensions', who deny they know exactly how improvement will occur, but nevertheless think they know what direction it must take. But, in the end, his judgment of them is the same:

> If you posit a single road, no matter how slowly you are prepared to move along it or how great the harvest you expect to gather as you go, you are a perfectionist, not because you know in detail what is at the end, but you have excluded every other road and are content with the certainty that perfection lies wherever it leads. And the office given to government in this enterprise is appropriate not only because of the amount of power it can exert but also because it needs to be exerted in one direction only. (*PFPS*)

It is typical of the politics of faith to assume that human power is sufficient to bring about a comprehensive condition fully satisfactory for human beings. Confidence in the capacity to travel the preferred road is essential:

> In the politics of Faith, political decision and enterprise may be understood as a response to an inspired perception of what *the* common good is, or it may be understood as the conclusion which follows a rational argument; what it can never be understood as is a temporary expedient or just doing something to keep things going. (*PFPS*)

Oakeshott distinguished the proclivity of the politics of faith for omnicompetent government from absolutism:

> A doctrine of absolutism, properly speaking, refers to the authorization of government. It implies a governing power ... authorized in such a manner that the authorization once given cannot, or cannot easily, be withdrawn, modified, transferred or otherwise interfered with; and perhaps ... also ... an authorization which bestows all ... power ... upon one person or body ... But this is something wholly different from an 'omnicompetent' government ... [which] refers not to authorization of government, but to the activity and objects in governing. For example, Hobbes may fairly be said to have understood government as the exercise of 'absolute' authority, and to be the first great theorist of sovereign government, but he shows no sign ... of understanding the activity of governing as an omnicompetent activity. There is absent from his pages any idea whatever of government as the agent of human improvement and perfection ... Government [for Hobbes] is paramount, but its activities are narrow ... [whereas] in the politics of Faith the activity of governing is understood as properly omnicompetent but not necessarily absolute ... [Nevertheless] this style of politics will be minute, inquisitive, and unindulgent: society will become a *panopticon* and its rulers *panoverseers* ... this concentration of effort ... will constitute government as the representative of the society in an enterprise of communal self-assertion whose purpose will be the spiritual, if not the physical, conquest of the world ... and a nice observance of rules and constitutions will readily be felt to hinder its impetus ... Moreover, it will be proper for an activity of governing wedded to the enterprise of perfection to require not merely obedience or submission from the subject, but approval and

> even love . . . the office of government will properly achieve a moral elevation which puts it above every other office. (*PFPS*)

No doubt those who are objects of this critique will insist that Oakeshott exaggerates grossly what they intend. Oakeshott agreed in acknowledging that he was setting forth an ideal type or an abstract extreme for analytical purposes, but he insisted that what he described shows the implicit logic of the politics of faith. How then does he set out the abstract extreme of the 'politics of Scepticism'?

In the first place, Oakeshott denies that one of these ideals was the cause of the other. That is, the politics of faith – in the modern sense of faith – did not come first and then produce a reaction against itself of a sceptical sort. Nor did the politics of scepticism appear because faith – in the old sense of the word faith – collapsed, thus eliciting the politics of faith in the new immanentist sense as an effort to retrieve us from spiritual crisis. These tendencies emerged coevally in the modern world in relation to the increasing power available to governments and the debate, persisting ever since, over whether it is more crucial to disperse or to aggregate that power.

The politics of scepticism rejects the pursuit of perfection. In modern times,

> the politics of scepticism (regarded as an abstract style of politics) may be said to have its roots either in the radical belief that human perfection is an illusion, or in the less radical belief that we know too little about the conditions of human perfection for it to be wise to concentrate our energies in a single direction . . . to pursue [perfection] as the crow flies . . . is to invite disappointment and . . . misery on the way. (*PFPS*)

In short, governing, according to the politics of scepticism, has no comprehensive purpose, and docs not claim to be in charge of a preferred manner of living that it encourages at the expense of alternatives:

> In this understanding of politics, then, the activity of governing subsists not because it is good, but because it is necessary. Its chief office is to lessen the severity of human conflict . . . the Sceptic understands order as a great and difficult achievement never beyond the reach of decay and dissolution. (*PFPS*)

At the same time, this order, while necessary, is not everything and we should endow it with only such resources as are needed to maintain it. The politics of scepticism is not opposed to strong government, but rather to expansive, omnicompetent aspirations in government. In Oakeshott's view, governing in this style is judicial activity not the pursuit of projects. After securing order, therefore, it is permissible

> to seek ... to improve the system of rights and duties and the concomitant system of means of redress, which together compose the superficial order ... Here what is to be improved is not human beings, or the conduct of human beings ... but the existing system of rights, duties and means of redress ... 'improvement' here is merely part of the articulation of maintaining order. (*PFPS*)

Oakeshott refers to this as the 'superficial order', conveying by that term the thought that there is a deeper, more comprehensive array of human relations which lives and moves and has its being apart from any governmental design, and which no government could ever finally subdue. Improvement in this context is equivalent to what Oakeshott means by maintaining order or, as he famously put it in his inaugural lecture, 'Political Education', attending to the arrangements of a set of people brought together by chance and choice. Maintenance is an interminable engagement because what is to be maintained

> has never been designed as a whole, and such coherence as it possesses is the product of constant readjustment of its parts to one another ... the system of superficial order is always capable of being made more coherent. To meditate upon this system and by replying to its intimations to make it more coherent is a manner of improving it which belongs (as the Sceptic understands it) to the office of government ... the barbarism of order appears when order is pursued for its own sake and when the preservation of order involves the destruction of that without which order is only the orderliness of the ant-heap or the graveyard ... The modest governor in this style does not consider himself better able than his neighbour to determine a general

> course of human activity. But . . . in his narrow business he can afford to be inexorable. (*PFPS*)

Oakeshott called himself a sceptic, one who would do better if only he knew how. As we have learned from recently published essays of his on the nature of philosophy,* he thought philosophy a subversive activity. He meant that philosophic appraisal of political positions clarifies them by explicating their animating assumptions in relation to the abstract ideals implied by those assumptions, without endorsing those assumptions or subscribing to the ideals. Philosophic appraisal shows what individuals assume, implicitly or explicitly, in order to understand themselves to be acting coherently, but it also brings out alternative assumptions which, if accounted for, would show incoherence. The appeals respectively in the politics of faith and in the politics of scepticism become clearer, and so do the limits of the styles in each case. The danger of the first is to overstate the possibilities of human action and to raise expectations beyond reason, the danger of the second is to understate the possibilities or, at any rate, the necessity of action and to be tardy in responding when action is called for. The sceptic, he said, thinks of government 'like garlic in cooking . . . [to be] so discreetly used that only its absence is noticed'. (*PFPS*)

In the actuality of modern European politics, 'government has occupied a middle region with only sporadic excursions to the horizons' but the two styles have shared a common vocabulary. For example, the famous expression, *salus populi suprema lex* is central to Western political discourse from the time of Cicero, and yet its meaning ranges

> from mere *safety* (relief from threatened extinction), through *health* (which is normal) and *prosperity* (which is modest), and *abundance* (which is excessive), and *welfare* (which is comprehensive), and on to *salvation* (which leaves nothing to be desired) . . . in the vocabulary of the Christian religion . . . salvation from sin . . . [and more recently] 'the public good', 'the public welfare', 'the prosperity of the nation' . . . 'the rule of righteousness'. (*PFPS*)

* *Michael Oakeshott on Religion, Politics and the Moral Life*, edited by Timothy Fuller, New Haven and London: Yale University Press, 1993.

Similarly, the meaning of 'the people' has gained a wide range of meanings, both inclusive and exclusive, and, for those who constitute the *populus*, *salus* could also mean 'rescued' or 'liberated'. And in modern talk about rights, we move from 'legal rights' to 'moral rights' to 'social rights' in daily discourse, and we move from the right to life, meaning protection from threats to survival, to the right to a certain standard of living, guaranteed by government, according to a repeatedly upwardly revised scale. People read into the vocabulary we use differing and conflicting connotations, often not noticing that this is the case.

In his philosophical scepticism, Oakeshott withheld himself from simply endorsing the politics of scepticism. The politics of scepticism, as a manifestation of the realm of practice, differs from philosophic scepticism which is the engagement to understand for the sake of understanding. The politics of scepticism is a form of practical action no less than the politics of faith, and cannot be content with understanding only, but must act.

Oakeshott's philosophical scepticism – which, as we have seen, need not oppose the traditional understanding of faith – continues the ancient philosophic tradition expressed in diverse idioms from Socrates to Hegel. Implicitly, Oakeshott is arguing that the politics of scepticism has an affinity with philosophic scepticism that differentiates it from the politics of faith, the distinctively modern experiment captured aphoristically in Marx's famous thesis on Feuerbach that the purpose is not to understand but to change the world. The connection must be implicit because Oakeshott, on his own terms, cannot deny the shaping presence of the alternative politics of 'faith'. Oakeshott's reflections on the character of modern politics restores, Socratically, an ancient insight to the debates of modern political life, and thus establishes by indirection the centrality of the conservative disposition in the history of political thought.

VII

WHOSE IS THIS IMAGE AND SUPERSCRIPTION? MONEY AND SOVEREIGNTY

RAY EVANS*

There is no greater political issue in the United Kingdom, indeed it has been the great issue for more than twenty years, than the relationship between the United Kingdom and Europe. This is particularly true for conservatives of the Oakeshottian school, amongst whom Shirley Letwin was the great interpreter. I believe it is no accident, then, that the culmination of the process of subordination, or submersion, of the United Kingdom into Europe, should be most powerfully symbolized with the creation of a European currency, a European central bank, and an end to the pound sterling, the French franc, the Italian lira, and at least in name, the Deutschmark.

At this point I should declare my interest in this debate. As an Australian anglophile I have viewed with very great distaste, from the very beginning, Britain's flirtation with, and then seduction by, what I regard as the European fantasy. It is with much satisfaction, then, that I observe the growing disenchantment of the British people with the European dream, and the increasing prospect that they will decide to get off that train which their leaders have warned them, so frequently, they must not fail to catch. That the issue which may trigger this disembarkation is 'money' means that we must inform ourselves about money and its relationship with the State.

My title is from Matthew 22:20. This famous text has provided

* Apart from the authors listed in the Notes I am much indebted over the years to George Fane of the Australian National University, John Greenwood of GT Management, Steve Hanke of Johns Hopkins University, Alan Reynolds of Hudson Institute, Richard Timberlake of University of Georgia, and Sir Alan Walters of AIG. Any errors of understanding are, naturally, wholly my own.

the basis for many arguments concerning the separation of church and State, and for at least one fine painting. Enoch Powell's translation* is

> But Jesus, perceiving their badness, said, 'Why do you try to trick me, you hypocrites? Show me the coinage of the tax.' They brought him a denarius, and he said to them, 'Whose is this likeness and superscription?' They said, 'Caesar's.' Then said he to them, 'So give Caesar what is Caesar's.'

My concern is with the connection, manifested by the emperor's head on the coin, between the State and the money which people use for their commercial transactions, large and small. Conservatives are always keenly interested in the well-being of the State (their own in particular). And because the State seems to be losing its authority, its well-being is, today, of particular concern.

Many conservatives have also been interested in money. Money is an institution which, like language and law, has evolved not through the conscious design of chattering class scribblers but through the experience gained as a result of many small innovations, by very many people, over a very long period of time. Numismatists are instinctive conservatives.

Very early in the evolution of Western civilization the State assumed monopoly control over issuance of coins. 'Lydia probably affords the best example of the state coining in this way. Tyranny as well as coinage are said to have originated there and the tyrant Gyges (687–652 BC) was probably responsible for making the right to coin precious metals a state monopoly.'**

The profits of seigniorage became a vital element of State income, along with customs duties and royalties from mining. Seigniorage is the difference between the cost of raw materials, gold, silver, copper or paper, together with the costs of manufacturing coins or notes, and the face value of the notes or coins issued. With paper notes there is a very large difference in seigniorage between notes which are not redeemable (fiat money) and those which are. Redeemable notes require the holding of reserves such as gold by the issuing bank, and that cost is significant. When the new Commonwealth

* J. Enoch Powell, *The Evolution of the Gospel*, 1994, Yale University Press, London.

** A. R. Burns, *Money and Monetary Policy in Early Times*, 1927, Kegan Paul, Trench, Trubner & Co, London, p. 83.

Government in Australia passed its Commonwealth Bank Notes Act in 1910 (which drove out private bank notes by imposing a 10 per cent tax on their face value) the private banks of the day did not fight the issue. They had made little profit from issuing notes. It was part of the bundle of financial services which they offered, but it was not one deemed worth fighting to retain.

Prior to bank notes the income from seigniorage increased greatly if the percentage of gold or silver in the coinage was reduced through alloying with base metals. Although by modern standards the profits from inflation, or depreciation of the currency, which accrued to the ancient and medieval princes who debased the coinage in this way, were very modest indeed, the practice was widely criticized at the time. Such debasement was only possible if the issuing authority could enforce acceptance of the coins at face value and this led to Gresham's law, which is much misunderstood. Gresham tells us that bad money drives out good. In other words people hoarded good coins and passed on inferior ones. However, this is only possible if refusal to accept the inferior money is a punishable offence.

The gravamen of my argument is that since the Second World War the abuse of their monopoly of monetary issue by States such as the United States and the United Kingdom has injured their citizenry, and has weakened their authority. Australia is similarly placed but its authority as a State, at home or abroad, has never been on the same scale as that of the United Kingdom. As an example of this monetary abuse I recall as a small schoolboy being given fourpence-halfpenny to buy a meat pie for lunch at a pie shop near the school. This was a very big treat. Today a meat pie usually costs two dollars or 240 old pence. In somewhat less than fifty years the nominal price of an Australian meat pie has increased 53-fold. I suspect similar examples could be found for the United Kingdom and the United States. Inflation data for the United Kingdom and Australia are given in Table 1.

The post-war inflation destroyed the pound sterling as a major world currency. In 1914 it was dominant on the world monetary stage. By the early 1950s it was seen as a sick currency, that is, a currency whose future value was extremely suspect, and this all too accurate perception carried over into the way British people and the Commonwealth, as it had become, saw Britain and its place in the

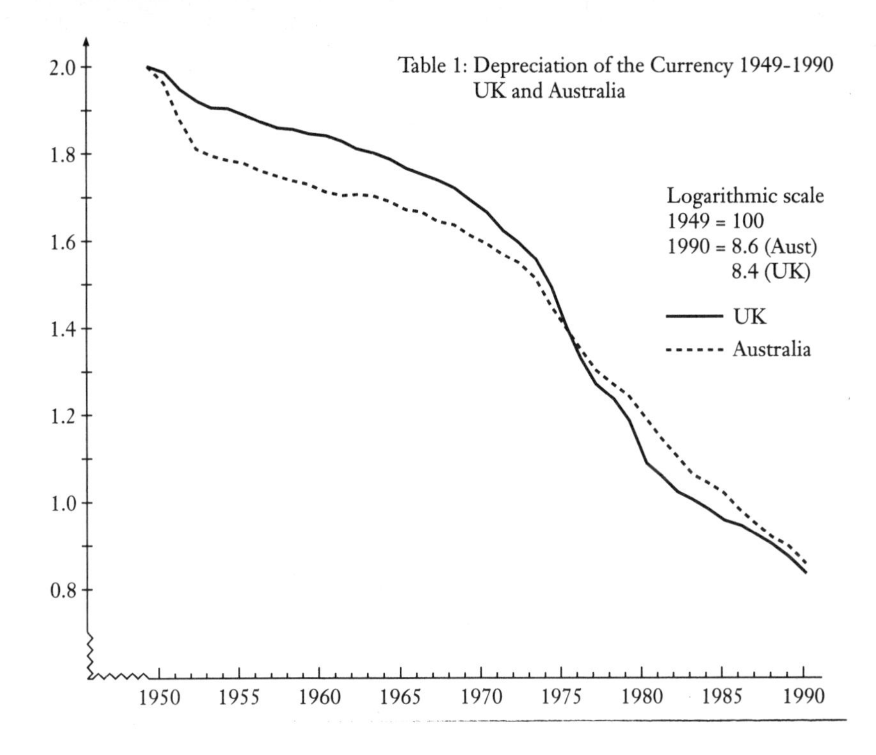

world. To my knowledge the most important conservative figure to understand the debilitating consequences of inflation and to preach against it during the 1950s and 60s was Enoch Powell, and his speeches, edited by John Wood,* provided me with an introduction to monetary issues. Powell had resigned his Treasury post in 1957 along with Thorneycroft and Birch over the size of the budget deficit, but at the time the connection between inflation and monetization of the deficit was not highlighted.

Thereafter Powell campaigned for a return to the gold standard but his major contribution, I believe, was to destroy the arguments which sought to blame the trade unions for inflation. He was obviously well aware of Friedman's contributions to monetary understanding, and his insistence that government, and government alone, was the culprit, was very important at that time.

* J. Enoch Powell, *Freedom and Reality*, edited by John Wood, 1969, B. T. Batsford Ltd, London.

Powell's position, to which he presumably still adheres, is that one of the State's most important duties, along with the defence of the realm and the preservation and refurbishment of our political institutions, is the issuance of sound, honest money for the citizenry. Furthermore he cast the argument in moral terms. Inflation was theft and for the State to steal from the citizenry, as a deliberate act of policy, inevitably led to dishonesty everywhere.

Sound, honest money is money which retains its purchasing power decade upon decade. This was certainly the experience of Britain from 1820 until the Great War. Beyond returning to the gold standard Powell did not offer any mechanisms through which the sovereign risk, characterized by unpredictable inflation, which by the 1960s closely attended most national currencies, was to be purged. (Sovereign risk is a term increasingly ubiquitous in the mining industry and refers to the propensities of sovereigns to renege on their contractual obligations, express or implied. Within the mining industry context sovereign risk is most graphically demonstrated when the State, having enticed exploration expenditure and investment on certain terms and conditions, expropriates ex post facto, in whole or in part, the discoverer of this new ore body. The Bank of England was established in 1694 as a device to provide credit for William and Mary, Charles II having spectacularly reneged on his debts in 1672, an historically important example of sovereign risk.)

In 1976 Hayek published his famous IEA monograph* on inflation and monetary reform. His important argument was that because of the intrinsic weaknesses of democratic political institutions, it was impossible for the State, at least in its contemporary form, to issue sound money and that private institutions would have to supplant the State in this role if we were ever to enjoy, again, the inestimable benefits which sound money provides.

Although I have no supporting evidence I presume that Powell would regard such a proposal as unthinkable. The connection between national sovereignty, and the currency of the realm, complete with the monarch's image on coins and notes, is so deeply

* Hayek wrote a number of papers on this subject, which became one of the main themes of his later years, among them *Denationalization of Money* (London: IEA, 1976) and *Denationalization of Money – The Argument Refined* (London: IEA, 1978).

rooted in the nation's history that a conservative, unlike a libertarian, will not entertain the abandonment of that connection.

In 1984 Laurence White published his important book on the history, and the theory, of the Scottish monetary and banking regime, extant from about 1740 to 1845, which we now characterize, rather unfortunately, as the outstanding example of 'free banking'.* This book was the beginning of an outpouring of books and papers which discussed and analysed the theory and practice of monetary regimes characterized by the absence of the sovereign risk which we now believe to be an inevitable feature of central banking regimes.

I have claimed that chronic post-war inflation has undermined the authority of the State. Michael Oakeshott wrote about the authority of the State as far back as 1929 and I read his essay, for the first time, just a few weeks ago. To my great satisfaction I found a sentence in that essay which suits my purposes exactly. 'The authority of the state is not mere government and law, nor is it founded upon a contract or any other form of the consent of the people, but resides solely in the completeness of the satisfaction which the state itself affords to the needs of concrete persons.'

For more than 2500 years the State has assumed responsibility for the provision of money. Money is an indispensable part of economic life. If it is to act effectively and properly as a store of value, a medium of exchange, and a unit of account, then it must, subject to minor qualifications, maintain its value over time and must not be subject to chronic but unpredictable depreciation. The State's reputation, as the monopoly supplier of money, must inevitably be affected by the quality of that money.

In our life-time we have become accustomed to thinking of the State as the compulsive debaucher of the currency. But this is a post-1930s phenomenon, at least in the English-speaking world. Shirley Letwin's most popular book, I believe, is her book on Trollope. Trollope took a very keen interest in economic life, as his book on his Australian and New Zealand travels well illustrates. Trollope is relevant to this paper because during his time the British Empire, at

* Laurence H. White, *Free Banking in Britain: Theory, Experience, and Debate, 1800–1845*, Cambridge: Cambridge University Press, 1984.

least by comparison with today, enjoyed a period of enviable monetary stability.

During the period 1870–1896, the pound sterling, along with all other gold-based currencies, increased gradually in purchasing power, and the period was known to economists of the day as the 'Great Depression'. It was a period of gentle deflation and was accompanied by very substantial economic growth and development, throughout the British Empire, and in the USA after the Civil War. This was the great era of the gold standard, and when France abandoned a silver standard in the 1870s most trading nations around the world were tied together at constant exchange rates through the commitment to a gold standard for their domestic currencies. Interest rates for consols typically provided 2–4 per cent over many decades and money increased in purchasing power by roughly 2 per cent, on average, per annum. This increasing purchasing power was driven by the slowly increasing relative price of gold.

An early point to be established is the contemporary nature of the State's monopoly. How is it that, apparently, we only have one currency in use in the United Kingdom (or in Australia) and that currency is the State-issued currency, with the Queen's head on notes and coin? The requirement that taxes are paid in coin (or notes) issued by the State is a significant part of the monopoly position which modern States have established in monetary issue. The contemporary State takes and spends nearly, or sometimes more, than half of the income earned by the citizenry, so the State's financial transactions dwarf all others. The other, very important, element of that monopoly power is the legal requirement that banks are compelled to use the State's money in their daily interbank settlement transactions, both with each other and with the central bank, acting as the government's bank.

In addition there is the very great convenience of a common currency which everyone uses, a convenience which provides a powerful aid towards the maintenance of a monopoly. Only in countries which have experienced the most debilitating inflations have other currencies contested the market. In Latin America, the former Soviet bloc, and Israel, the United States dollar became, either openly or covertly, the currency used for secret or major transactions. So much so that it has been estimated that between 40 and 80 per cent of the

United States note issue is held outside the United States. Perhaps some of that money is now being repatriated, or converted to yen.

Not only are large stocks of United States notes held outside the United States but the Euro-dollar market, now one of the world's largest and most successful financial markets, and entirely unregulated by any sovereign, provides an example of the ingenuity of market players to build a very large enterprise on small foundations. I understand the Euro-dollar market was built up, in its earliest days, on United States dollar deposits issued by European banks to the Soviet government. The USSR did not wish to locate such deposits within reach of the United States government, but nevertheless wished to have access to United States dollar accounts, in order, amongst other things, to fund espionage.

The concept of legal tender and the explicit monopoly rights embodied therein now seems to have all but vanished. The theory of legal tender was that the courts would not uphold a contract if settlement of debts took place using a method of payment other than the coin of the realm – the State's own money. This doctrine was so greatly at variance with the fundamental principles of contract law that it could not endure.

The material we wish to consider, then, is this:

the great contrast between the pound sterling in Trollopean times and since the Second World War;

the close connection between the proposed demise of the pound sterling and the end of British sovereignty as we have known it for hundreds of years;

the monetary institutions, particularly central banks, which, in their various ways, operate the State's monetary monopoly;

what changes a State such as the United Kingdom or Australia might introduce to restore sound money and sovereign reputation.

This is a very large topic indeed. A number of important books and papers on monetary and banking theory have been written in recent years and the debate continues vigorously between those who maintain the necessity of central banks and those who regard them as just another government monopoly which necessarily brings about monetary instability.* For the purposes of this paper I will focus on what I see as a key issue in this debate – the distinction between price and quantity in relation to monetary issue.

When Margaret Thatcher assumed office in 1979 she was regarded as, and often attacked for being, a monetarist. Sometimes the adjective 'heartless' was appended to the label. Underlying these attacks was the assumption that she believed that the quantity of money issued by the Bank of England was central to inflation outcomes. Attention was then focused on changes in M0, M1, M3 or M2 or whatever monetary aggregates were in fashion at the time and whether or not these measures could guide central banks in the discharge of their duties.

I think one can conclude from her autobiography** that the Prime Minister did share a belief, in an intuitive way, in these quantity theories. Regardless of that there can be no argument that Mrs Thatcher believed that inflation was dangerous and destructive, economically, morally and socially, and that it had to be stopped. And she succeeded during the first five or six years of her prime ministership in reducing inflation to post-war lows.

David Glasner has pointed out in his perceptive and illuminating book*** that concern about the quantity of money in circulation goes back to David Hume and his arguments concerning the substitution of paper (banknotes) for gold, which he believed to be highly inflationary. Adam Smith, contrariwise, argued that competition between note-issuing banks, and the convertibility of those banknotes into gold would, as contemporary Scottish experience demonstrated, provide stable prices and reliable banks. Hume was the founder of the quantity theory of money whereas Smith focused on price.

> The increase of paper money, it has been said, by augmenting

* For an excellent summary of the battle between the protagonists for free banking and defenders of central banks from the viewpoint of a central bank protagonist, see the article by Charles Goodhart, 'The Free Banking Challenge to Central Banks' in *Critical Review*, Vol. 8, No 3, Summer 1994.

** Margaret Thatcher, *The Downing Street Years*, London: HarperCollins, 1993, Chapter XXIV.

*** David Glasner, *Free Banking and Monetary Reform*, 1989, Cambridge University Press, pp. 51–6.

> the quantity, and diminishing the value of the whole currency, necessarily augments the money price of commodities. But as the quantity of gold and silver, which is taken from the currency, is always added to the quantity of paper which is added to it, paper money does not necessarily increase the quantity of the whole currency.*

Adam Smith could have added that it would not have mattered if it did. The demand for currency, and therefore its supply, might well have increased when paper replaced gold. Paper is certainly easier to carry. But as long as the value of the bank-notes was determined by the convertibility of those notes at the Newtonian rate of 113 grains to the pound the only possible cause of change in purchasing power of the currency would have been changes in the relative price of gold.

That Scottish banking and monetary regime was tragically destroyed by Peel's Bank Charter Acts of 1844 and 1845, the consequence of 'a combination of rent-seeking by established bankers and dubious theoretical arguments by monetary economists'.** The Bank of England developed thereafter as the world's most important central bank (at least until the First World War), albeit constrained by the statutory requirement to limit its note issue and to maintain gold backing and convertibility.

Discussion of monetary quantities or aggregates is only possible within a monopoly regime. A central bank can keep tabs on MO (bank-notes plus other central bank liabilities such as CDs) or on 'settlement cash' (used by the banks for interbank settlements) and since all other monetary aggregates are pyramided on MO, economists can produce lagged correlations between whichever M takes their fancy and inflation, until retirement.

But since the 1980s, as inflation became widely recognized as a political liability, and as any sustained relationship between the various Ms and inflation was never demonstrated in practice, central bank attention moved from tracking monetary aggregates to the purchasing power of the currency under their control. That purchasing power is the price of the currency. The price almost always under

* From *The Wealth of Nations* quoted by Glasner, *ibid*, pp. 54–5.

** Laurence H. White, 'Which Kind of Monetary Policy, If Any?' *Cato Journal*, Vol. 13, No 2, p. 198.

consideration is the bundle of prices aggregated within the CPI and, as in the New Zealand Reserve Bank Act, the doctrine is that inflation, as measured by the Consumer Price Index (CPI), or CPI minus interest rate changes, is to be kept within a statutory range, typically 0–2 per cent per annum.

Since the money central banks issue is not contractually redeemable or convertible by the issuers to anything but itself or, through the foreign exchange markets, to fiat currencies issued by other central banks, the mechanisms employed to maintain a low inflation regime are necessarily complex. The instrument now widely used is variation of interest rates, a form of price control, and the result is that the Australian press, for example, is full of chatter concerning what the Reserve Bank is going to do with interest rates when the next State election is over, or the next Balance of Payments data is published. Australian interest rates are always priced in relation to the US interest rate and currently it is about two and a half full points above that. Share values, housing prices, and above all bond values, go up and down on the strength of these rumours.

Leland Yeager focused on exchange rate volatility when he summarized the sovereign risk now associated with interest rate and exchange rate manipulation in these words:

> It seems absurd to let so pervasively influential a price as a country's exchange rate jump around in response to investors' and speculators' changeable whims about their asset holdings. It seems absurd that changes in, and expectations and rumours about, monetary and fiscal policies, trade policies and market interventions should be allowed to exert such quick, magnified, and pervasive effects. But we should be clear about just *what* is absurd.
>
> It is not the flexibility of exchange rates. It is not the alleged free-market determination of prices on the exchange markets. The absurdity consists, rather, in what those prices are the prices *of*. They are the prices of national fiat moneys expressed in each other, each lacking any defined value.
>
> The value of each money depends on conjectures about the good intentions of the government issuing it and perceptions about its ability to carry through on its good intentions. These

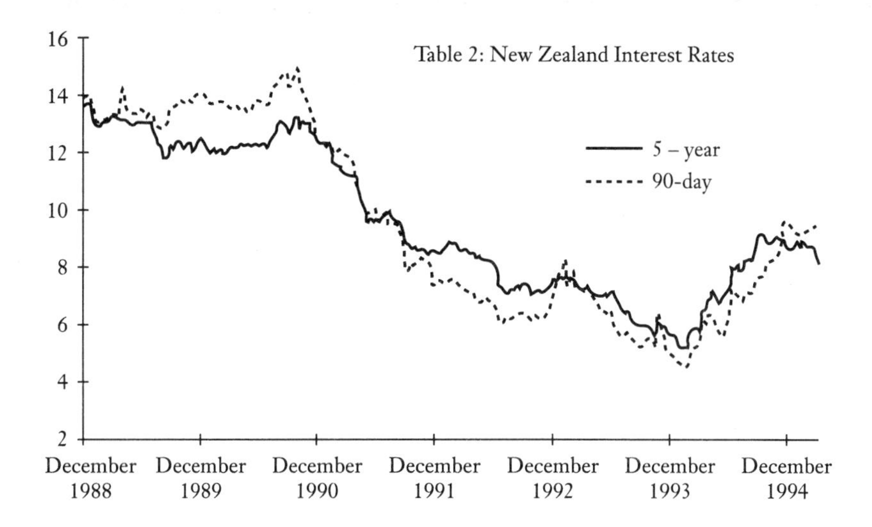

conjectures and perceptions are understandably subject to sharp change.*

Most central banks today rely entirely on controlling short-term interest rates to achieve whatever monetary ambitions they may entertain at a particular time in the ebb and flow of political and economic life. As in Australia and New Zealand, they may use the amount of money they make available for day by day interbank settlements as a mechanism for producing the interest rate regime they wish to obtain. But regardless of technique the markets and the banks focus on interest rates and their future course as a guide to their own decision making.

This creates very great instability. In 1989, Australian overnight rates reached nearly 20 per cent, and mortgagees were paying 20 per cent on house loans. Small businesses were going bankrupt at an alarming rate. Some large corporations went belly up. The recent history of New Zealand interest rates (by no means the worst) is given in Table 2.

All of this is a consequence of central bank monopoly, the attendant sovereign risk which is a necessary consequence of State monopoly,

* Leland B. Yeager, 'The Significance of Monetary Disequilibrium', *Cato Journal* 6, Fall 1986.

and the inevitable ignorance on the part of the monopolist of the consequences of his actions in manipulating interest rates in order to produce either an inflation outcome or an exchange rate outcome.

The experience of Scotland from about 1740 to 1845, the Australian experience from 1830 to 1910, (amongst others)* and the Euro-dollar experience of recent years tell us beyond fear of contradiction that it is possible to have a stable monetary and banking regime without a central bank. Our recent experience indicates very strongly that we would be better off without a central bank, even a German central bank. The key issue to be decided in the abandonment of central banking is the price rule which must control the competitive issuing of bank-notes.

When we have many banks issuing pound notes there is no control, other than the clearing house at which the banks exchange their notes with each other, over the quantity of money in circulation. The much discussed monetary aggregates lose their meaning, at least in the sense of providing a control mechanism. What does matter is the price at which these bank-notes can be converted to some more widely accepted medium of exchange. Under the gold standard a pound note could be redeemed, on demand, with 113 grains of fine gold. This was the price rule which governed the operation of the Scottish and later the Australian banking systems, which performed very well without a central bank.

If banks are to issue their own notes then a price rule has to be employed, and considerable attention has focused on a suitable monetary price rule for our times. Gold has largely fallen out of favour; perhaps Keynes' famous accusation, 'a barbarous relic' has stuck. Kevin Dowd, the leading British free banking advocate, said this of a gold price rule:

> The gold standard may or may not deliver a more predictable price level than a continuation of the present fiat system, but it is still the case that one of the main arguments against a

* Vera C. Smith, *The Rationale of Central Banking and the Free Banking Alternative*, England: P. S. King & Son, 1936, republished by Liberty Press, Indianapolis, 1990, preface by Leland Yeager; Kevin Dowd (ed.), *The Experience of Free Banking*, London and New York: Routledge, 1992; Kevin Dowd, *Laissez-faire Banking*, London and New York: Routledge, 1993.

> restoration of the gold standard is the price level uncertainty that would arise because no one can predict the future relative price of gold with any high degree of confidence.*

Because gold was not looked upon with favour, some economists busied themselves constructing baskets of commodities which would provide a suitable price rule in lieu of gold. One such basket was Hall's (1982) ANCAP basket – a basket of specified amounts of ammonium nitrate, copper, aluminium and plywood. This basket had shown purchasing power stability over the period 1950–1980. But the problem about any basket of commodities which might be given legal status as the determinants of a price rule is that the behaviour of market participants regarding these commodities will change dramatically, once they are given monetary status.

Most of the discussion concerning inflation, and the establishment of a monetary regime which will eliminate sovereign risk with respect to money, has taken for granted that the proper price rule is a zero inflation rule as determined by the CPI – the consumer price index. Kevin Dowd, for example, has argued for a monetary regime in which price stability, that is, zero change to the CPI, is achieved through central bank issuance of a new kind of financial instruments, 'similar but not identical to a price index futures contract'. This instrument 'would promise the holder a payment on maturity that was contingent on the "announced" value of a price index on that date'.**

The basic idea is that if people begin to suspect that monetary policy is too loose then they will convert cash into these promissory notes and thus withdraw base money from circulation. This will immediately reduce inflationary pressures.

Other reformers do not support a price stabilization rule. George Selgin is one of the contemporary protagonists for free banking who has argued for a different regime:

> Although price-level stabilization is the only widely endorsed price-level policy today, there was a time when prominent economists from numerous schools favoured a different approach – the 'productivity norm' of price-level behaviour. Under this

* Kevin Dowd, *A Rule to Stabilize the Price Level*, Unpublished MS, October 1993.
** Kevin Dowd, 'A Proposal to End Inflation', in *Economic Journal*, 104 (425) 1994, pp. 828–40.

> approach the consumer price level is allowed to vary inversely with changes in unit real costs of production. In theory, the productivity norm is equivalent to stabilization of a price index of factors of production: In practice it is roughly equivalent to the stabilization of per capita nominal income.*

In other words average weekly earnings, under such a price rule, would remain approximately the same from generation to generation, as they did indeed during the latter part of the Victorian era. But, of course, under such a regime, the price of most commodities, particularly manufactured commodities, would be in a state of gradual but continuous decline.

Selgin argues that under a central bank regime such a productivity-norm could be readily approximated by the central bank adopting a policy of 'directly stabilizing some readily available measure of the flow of money payments or income such as nominal GDP or domestic final demand'.**

However, once a central bank is required to implement a price rule we are back to the problem of the capacity to know what nominal GDP or some other monetary measure really is. In Australia, as elsewhere, GDP figures are revised months and sometimes years after they are first released. And, once again, the only conceivable instrument for influencing price levels is through control and manipulation of interest rates.

Selgin, however, has also noted, 'As an empirical matter I do believe that a free-banking gold standard would most likely lead to something like a "productivity norm" rather than "zero inflation" in practice, as happened in gold standard countries throughout the last half of the nineteenth century.'***

The argument now boils down to something like this. Central banks, in conjunction with their political masters have, for more than sixty years, played havoc with money and have caused great personal hardship and political instability. There seems no reason to believe that anything has happened which will give us confidence that central

* George Selgin, 'Monetary Equilibrium and the Productivity Norm of Price Level Policy', in *Cato Journal*, Vol. 10, No 1, 1990.

** *Ibid.*

*** George Selgin, correspondence, 1992.

banks will perform in a radically different manner than hitherto, the New Zealand experience notwithstanding. Current exchange rate instability is very strong evidence on this point.

The only conceivable alternative to central bank monopoly is competitive note issue by banks, which under current circumstances will have some sort of licence from the State to issue deposits and notes, and conduct other financial services. Under such a regime of competitive note issue, a price rule must be adopted and convertibility of bank-notes to some more widely accepted form of money (high-powered money) has to be guaranteed.

Although zero inflation (as measured by the CPI) is usually assumed to be the only conceivable monetary rule which should guide those who issue money, other rules are worthy of consideration, notably a productivity-norm or constant per capita nominal income rule.

Whilst a number of mechanisms for establishing a price rule either of the zero inflation or the productivity-norm kind have been proposed, all of them, save the gold price rule or a commodity basket price rule, are exceedingly complex and depend upon the use and accuracy of official statistics such as CPI, or GDP, or variants of them.

A gold price rule, in which the pound sterling, for example, is defined as *y* grains of gold would, as Selgin argues, provide a good approximation to a productivity-norm price rule.

A monetary regime embodying these principles for the pound sterling (or the Australian dollar) would encompass the following:

1. Abolition of the requirement that interbank settlements (within the United Kingdom) use the pound sterling. This would mean an end to interest rate control by the central bank.
2. The Crown contracts with banks at home and abroad to issue bank-notes denominated in pounds sterling, complete with the monarch's portrait and with designs approved by the Crown, on condition that such notes are to be convertible into the equivalent weight of gold *or an accepted substitute* within a stipulated and acceptable period of time.

In my view such a monetary regime would find ready and widespread acceptance. It would quickly lead to the emergence of the pound sterling as a strong world currency. It would certainly throw a spanner in the works of the Europhiles and make it clear that the United Kingdom was not going to accept European monetary union.

In the forthcoming debates concerning European monetary union much ink will be spilt on the value which will accrue to the participants under a European central bank run by the Germans. In these debates it will be important to be able to master the elements of monetary theory and be able to contest these arguments. At the same time the future of the pound sterling has to be on the agenda. In this paper I have attempted to set out the elements of a political program of monetary reform which would enable a British government to take the initiative in these important matters. It does not, for an instant, pretend to be the last word, but I commend the basic idea as relevant to conservatives who regard the State as vital to civilized life as we know it, who value the achievements of the past, and wish to use those achievements to solve the political and economic problems of the present.

VIII

UNREALISM AND FOREIGN POLICY: RUSSIA AND THE MIDDLE EAST

DAVID PRYCE-JONES

Settled Life is a phrase which recurs with approval in the writings of Elie Kedourie. In the main he was referring specifically to the four centuries of Ottoman rule, during which Arabs, as Ottoman subjects, had enjoyed a peace not experienced at any other period of their history. It was a despotism, to be sure, but right up to 1914 no Arab had cause to suppose that *backward* was a description that could be applied to him and his existence. Throughout the world of Islam, as indeed in Asia and Africa, the historic tradition of one-man rule was characterized and tempered by religion, custom, clan and tribal loyalty. To Kedourie, the associated practices and beliefs were guide-ropes to secure essential culture and identity. Since change was certain, wisdom in government consisted in ensuing that it was neither undue nor unnecessary. Change for its own sake deranged the whole order. Those living a settled life had no need to ask themselves the existential question, Who am I?

The effect of Western expansion was to ram that question in the face of millions of people in a manner which insisted upon an answer. Conquest had been part of their historic experience; inferiority had not. Hospitals, schools, communications, impartial administration, were dependent upon a State structure, that whole complex of institutions and supporting values which provide government by consent. Here apparently was the key to Western dynamism and the changes that accompanied it. But what appeared self-evidently beneficial to Westerners were alien impositions to others. An insoluble puzzle, out of which the Third World has taken its disturbed shape.

In innumerable memoirs the likes of Ho Chi Minh, Chou En-Lai, Nehru and Gandhi, Michel Aflaq (the founder of Baathism), Habib Bourguiba, Jomo Kenyatta and Kwame Nkrumah have described themselves poring over books in Paris and London to investigate this puzzle on behalf of themselves and, as they liked to suppose, their people. Once the question Who am I? is out in the open, the response has to be, *Someone at least as good as you.* It was easy enough to draw the conclusion that in their dealings with other people Westerners were not living up to the standards implicit in their own institutions and supporting values. A nationalist movement was a repudiation of backwardness or inferiority. Very little violence was needed to convince Westerners to fall in with this. Withdrawing with whatever grace they could muster, former Western rulers handed over such State structures as they had managed to create. Too embryonic for government by consent, or too remote to be applicable, the whole alien imposition was almost immediately swallowed back into the historic tradition of one-man rule, converting into the new instrument of oppression. By that point, settled life had become a thing of the past, had lost its protectiveness, was even a cause for shame. Nothing stood between the ambition of the new ruler and the subjection of the ruled.

For incoming power-holders, ruling in the circumstances was an act of pure will. Taking advantage of what they had seized, appropriating all available resources, the first generation of power-holders in Islamic, African and Asian countries arranged the State to suit themselves, like so many Louis XIVs with his *L'état c'est moi*. Another generation, and the alternative has been clarified; either such a country has a despot brutal enough to enforce his will and keep the peace of the graveyard, or it disintegrates into constituent ethnic components, tribes, sects and other minority groupings. In examples like Liberia, Sierra Leone, Somalia, Sudan, Burundi and Rwanda, Lebanon, Afghanistan, Cambodia and many more, government has disintegrated to the extent that quite simple acts of administration, sometimes even the acceptance of foreign aid, are beyond its capacities.

So far only two European countries, Russia and Yugoslavia, have landed in this predicament. In terms of natural resources, Russia is far and away the richest country in the world; its catastrophe is entirely man-made, deliberate.

Historic Russia had been a classic, indeed oriental, despotism in which ruling was a process of attempting to centralize and concentrate power in a single hand. Russian Orthodoxy had maintained the essential culture and identity. Marx and Lenin had also pored over books in foreign libraries, and their doctrine substituted the proletariat for the Tsar: a play with words, since despotism remained constant. In destroying Tsarism, the incoming Communist Party was like an early version of a post-colonial regime. The primitive previous State structure was easily absorbed into the new repressive mechanism. It claimed to be a popular mass party while ensuring that government by consent was excluded from the political process. The party contained within itself the State. The usual description of the Soviet Union as a party-state was a tautology. The executive, legislative and judiciary were only branches of the party in which members could be drafted at will for the sole purpose of extending the monopoly of power. The party cherished this monopoly by distributing privileges and rewards as it saw fit within the elite, or the nomenklatura. Mamelukes or janissaries provide the appropriate historic parallel.

Catching up and overtaking the West was the ostensible purpose of the party's endeavours. Every general secretary criticized the alleged backwardness of the past. Fear of the stigma of inferiority was unmistakable. Here was the motivation for the cold-blooded and murderous determination with which the party turned on the population. History has no example to match the savagery of the communists towards people who were their own kind. Far the greater part of them shared their ethnic origins and culture. A thousand years of peasant life, and the religion which had sustained it, were uprooted. Culture and morality were defined as whatever served the party's ends. Voluntary association down to the most educational and self-sacrificing levels became a criminal offence. The country was swept bare.

This mystification of tyranny as progress made the Soviet Union an attractive model to post-colonial power-holders. Self-imposed tyranny could be presented as modernizing, catching up with the West, avoiding shame about backwardness. A Soviet-style single party simulated popular consent. What was new was not the cruelty but the sustained assault against settled life. Nothing remained of it in countries which fell under Soviet sway; even Egypt and Ethiopia with age-old identities were lost in the grip of the single party, the secret police and the concentration camp.

Granted its stranglehold on the population, the Soviet party-state could have lasted more or less indefinitely in Russia or elsewhere. Appointed general secretary in 1985, Mikhail Gorbachev was a true believer, and remains one today, as he muses over the strange process whereby his touch brought down everything which he stood for. In a view which he shared with every previous general secretary, the party had failed to wring out of the population an industrial performance strong enough to underpin the military and political expansion which proved the truth of the doctrine and justified the monopoly of power. In the party-state, purging was the sole mechanism available for change, its function was akin to elections in a democracy. Nobody could forget the methods by which Stalin had obtained the party for the ends he chose. Perestroika, or reform, was well understood as the euphemism for the sort of purging which follows from the general secretary's aspiration to maximize power. It seemed no great harm to Gorbachev and his advisors to eliminate elderly nomenklatura members by changing the rubber-stamp Soviet parliament into the Congress of People's Deputies. Designed neither as a legislature nor a debating chamber, this Congress was intended to provide a screen which would pass as popular consent. By way of a safeguard, the majority of deputies were party nominees but it was possible for candidates to run against one another, although all were party members. For the first time an element of competition had been introduced into the party-state.

In itself this might not have mattered. In an absolute despotism, power does not pass from one holder to the next through an institution but because of the death or destruction of the incumbent. A challenger has to be strong and convincing enough to be allowed into the inner circle, while also clever and cunning enough to conceal his ambitions. In their different ways, Gorbachev and Boris Yeltsin exemplified this do-or-die business: the former confident or oblivious enough to promote the latter, only to discover that he had raised a rival against himself. Failing to eliminate or at least to neutralize Yeltsin as all previous general secretaries would have done, Gorbachev either misunderstood or mishandled the monopoly of power. In his turn, Yeltsin perceived that the new-fangled Congress of People's

Deputies offered him an opportunity to transfer his fight away from the secrecy of the Kremlin out into the open. He had an arena in which to plead that the raising of his standard in revolt was really a turn towards government by consent. As when Stalin put millions to death out of suspicion of Trotsky's ambitions, so now the Gorbachev–Yeltsin rivalry contained the germ of civil war. The very element of electoral competitiveness that had vitalized this germ afresh fortunately also opened up enough of a political process to head off bloodshed. The civil war, when it came to a head in August 1991, became a formality, a consummate piece of theatre, staged to test out where the balance of power lay. The stakes had risen so high that Gorbachev and Yeltsin had been equally willing to rearrange the Soviet Union, Russia, the party, nationalism, communism, democracy and the free market and the Cold War and anything else in pursuit of victory.

The surprise which these events aroused in the West was extreme, deriving as it did from decades of denial of reality. Fellow-travelling was altogether one of the most peculiar intellectual phenomena of this century: a complexity fed by many underground streams of guilt, fear and frustration, alienation, admiration of power, misplaced idealism. It may never be possible to explain fully why so many Westerners, who themselves enjoyed government by consent, apologized for government by violence elsewhere. Not only Soviet reality was denied. Western commentary often glossed over the fact that independence and democracy in the Third World was a nightmare of corruption, massacre and abuse of power.

To be sure, the United States and its allies had since the days of the Truman administration maintained a defensive alliance against the Soviet Union, but the cost of rolling back Soviet expansion and thus winning the Cold War had always been considered prohibitive. Public opinion never whole-heartedly approved the anti-communism of President Reagan and Mrs Thatcher, while the Star Wars programme remained controversial to the end. By contrast the Campaign for Nuclear Disarmament, with its *Better red than dead* slogan, détente, peaceful coexistence, liberation theology, Euro-Communism, Ostpolitik, the SALT and START treaties, are among the manifestations of Western inventiveness when it came to appeasing the Soviet Union.

A milestone on the route was the 1975 Helsinki Conference. At it, the United States and thirty-three European States had signed what was known as the Final Act which guaranteed the *territorial integrity of states* in Europe. The Red Army's military conquest of Eastern and Central Europe was thus legitimized. The forceful incorporation of the Baltic Republics into the Soviet Union was swept under the carpet. No longer simply an emanation of Soviet power, East Germany became a state recognized in its own right. To the likes of Brezhnev, Erich Honecker and General Jaruzelski, we have subsequently learned, the Helsinki Final Act appeared to acknowledge the moment when the balance of power had finally swung towards communism and against the West. The readiness with which the West had accepted Gorbachev's description of the 1970s as the *years of stagnation* demonstrated how false perceptions were internalized as true simply on the Soviet say-so. In 1987 Honecker was received in West Germany as a head of state on an official visit – two years later he was put on trial there. President Bush supported Gorbachev in his attempts to prop up communism rather than Yeltsin who had no choice but to sign its death certificate. Even at the actual death bed in the summer of 1991, President Bush did not condemn Gorbachev's blockade of the Baltics, and he warned Ukraine against its aspiration to be independent. Only weeks later he was claiming, *We won the Cold War*. This was an illusion. Dissolving as the result of an improbable series of accidents and the improvisations of its internal power struggle, the Soviet Union had released itself and everyone else from the Cold War.

Without the party there was no State either. Russia today is more of a large inhabited area than a country. Yeltsin had wanted revenge and power, but he had not anticipated that in obtaining them he would have to deny the party-state which had made him what he was, and to which he owed everything. Having manipulated the opening afforded by the Congress of People's Deputies in order to present himself as a democrat and a nationalist, he could not then revert to type. Like any Third World ruler seizing power in the imperial aftermath, a zero hour of his own making, he had to improvise from scratch administrative structures to replace the party and the State. Experts drafted for him a constitution suitable for a strong president and a weak Duma but there was neither a state structure nor an administrative machinery to translate the paper work into effective law. Yeltsin's writ carries hardly further than the sound of his voice. In the political and social vacuum which is Russia, it is every man for himself, a kind of civilian version of the criminality which was formerly the privileged monopoly of the party. A quite unprecedented free-for-all level has been reached in which the contents of national museums and libraries, state secrets, materials for nuclear weaponry, the whole process of privatization, are looted and exploited without hindrance and nobody is brought to answer for it. The Third World choice between brutal despotism and disintegration has engulfed the Soviet Union and its successor States. Turkmenistan and Kazakhstan and Uzbekistan are among those States which have reverted to one man-rule, while others like Tajikistan, Armenia, Azerbaijan, Georgia, are at the mercy of warring bands and ethnic groups asserting themselves. A construct every bit as wilful and therefore fragile, the Yugoslav party and the Yugoslav State have also foundered together. Former Soviet satellites in East and Central Europe have escaped this fate only in so far as the party had not had time enough to wipe out historic culture and identity, and settled life was still a living memory.

Whatever slogans he may mouth, Yeltsin, in the manner of his predecessors in the Kremlin, has been obliged to resort to force. In pursuit of open imperial hankerings, he has ordered troops into several former Soviet republics nominally independent, and he has secured with his border-guards the former Soviet boundaries everywhere except the Baltic States. *The near abroad* which he now says is Russia's legitimate foreign policy sphere happens to coincide with the Soviet bloc. Internally he has shelled the Duma building, arresting his own vice-president and other parliamentarians who had raised the standard of revolt against him as he had raised it against Gorbachev. He has ordered the invasion of Chechnya, with the destruction by bombing and heavy artillery of its larger towns. Far more casualties have resulted from this one punitive expedition alone than there were altogether in the years under Gorbachev. Half a century after Stalin's mass deportation, Chechens are once again being exiled to Siberia.

Without a state structure there can be no settled life, but without settled life no state structure seems able to evolve. Yeltsin has to find a way out of this bind. Should he succeed, his example will serve half the world's countries which are in a similar plight. For a conservative realist, the question is whether a despotism can create conditions of settled life, and if so, how. As Kedourie stressed, the introduction of Western democratic values and practices has already been tried and found wanting. But in Third World upheavals, as in the collapse of the Soviet Union, there has been a central thrust, however erratic and incoherent, to introduce the element of consent. Islamic fundamentalism is certainly one attempt along these lines but that project is doomed because it rests upon idealization of a long-ago past when religion itself was held to be all that was needed by way of a state structure.

Meanwhile to depict Yeltsin and his Russia as democratic and making a brave attempt to substitute law for the party, thus worthy of support and IMF loans, is another denial of reality, what may be called post-communist fellow-travelling.

Within the democracies of Western Europe another project is underway, to merge into a federal union – and beyond that, a unitary State perhaps – a number of societies hitherto differentiated by language, law, religion, political and social institutions and customs. Here is another act of pure will on the part of a very limited number of politicians. Accountable to no electorates, an embryonic state structure is in the process of formation. Whether or not they wish for it, whole populations once again are to be improved in the name of centralization and modernization. To stay as they are is allegedly backward. The whole world is said to be divided into competitive trading blocs in which membership is a matter of geo-historical determination. Whether federation really brings the alleged benefits of peace, increased trade and higher living standards is shrouded in obfuscating nomenklatura-type language, mystifying motives and justifications alike.

The modalities of federal union are discussed and decided behind doors almost as closed as were those of the Kremlin. Some of the countries apparently set to participate have held referendums, but these have been framed to suit preordained ends, and simply reversed upon results unsatisfactory to the framers. Absence of genuine democratic consent introduces confusion and conflict, even an ultimate prospect of armed enforcement or collapse, in an uncanny Western echo of the Soviet experiment. Pending clarification of this alternative, national parliaments and law-making and law-enforcing bodies are being weakened. What had been considered independent state structures can no longer be taken for granted. What does *settled life* signify in the context? Is this not the introduction of change for its own sake? Compliance is therefore dropping out of the social order in the countries of Europe, to be replaced by crime and corruption, cultural loss and anomie already characteristic of Russia and the rest of the Third World. The gathering challenge to identity is breeding the false defences of fascism and racism. People turn violent once they are invited to answer the question *Who am I?* with *Nobody much*.

IX

DOES REALISM HAVE A FUTURE?

OWEN HARRIES

All conservative speakers have to invoke Edmund Burke at some point. I'll do so right at the beginning. In his great speech on conciliation with America, Burke reflected sombrely on the difficulties of communicating across the Atlantic: 'Three thousand miles of ocean lie between you and them. No contrivance can prevent the effect of this distance in weakening government. Seas roll, and months pass, between the order and the execution, and the want of a speedy explanation of a single point is enough to defeat a whole system.'

I have to report that, despite the subsequent introduction of the telephone and the fax, Kenneth Minogue and I contrived to duplicate some of these difficulties in the run-up to this conference. The exchange of information was sketchy and slow.

I mention this because I suspect that I haven't produced quite the paper that Ken expected, the right paper for the occasion. But there you are. As Burke must have said to the electors of Bristol on more than one occasion: you win some, you lose some.

It is only in the realm of international politics that realism has been developed into a full-blown political doctrine. In so far as this paper has a theme, it centres on the question: How does a political doctrine that puts all its money on continuity fare in a period of rapid, arguably profound, change?

Realism assumes that the basic conditions of international politics are self-perpetuating, immutable. These conditions, as you know, include, first, a human nature that contains a large component of selfishness, competitiveness and the will to dominate; second, States that possess a virtual monopoly of military power and are far and away the most important players in international politics; and, third, the state of anarchy in which these States, each insisting on its sovereignty, coexist.

Realists recognize that change occurs, of course, but maintain that, as long as these three conditions persist, other changes, however dramatic they might seem, are of secondary importance and leave the game of power politics essentially in place. Realism offers no theory of systemic change, and dismisses as utopian proposals that claim to be able to bring such change about.

Until now, this way of going on has served realists well, and they have had much the better of the argument with those who put their faith in the forces of sweeping change. The three conditions they identify as fundamental have remained more or less constant for a very long time, and so has the behaviour of the actors in international politics. Kissinger writes about the same kind of activities that Thucydides wrote about.

What are the reasons, then, for believing that this may now be changing? Well, the end of the Cold War has revitalized various forms of hopes and expectations, expectations that were partially suppressed and subordinated to what used to be known as 'hard-nosed realism' while the conflict was on. After four decades of such realism it is not surprising that when that conflict ended there was a marked reaction. Actually, the *way* that the Cold War ended may have contributed to this reaction, because it seemed to contradict the tenets of realism. As the leading English realist, Martin Wight, once put it, 'Great Power status is lost, as it is won, by violence. A Great Power does not die in its bed.' But that seemed to be precisely what the Soviet bear did under Gorbachev. Sick, it tried various cures, pined and died. Whether this was the aberrant behaviour of an aberrant State or a sign of things to come is a question still to be addressed.

That apart, the end of the Cold War generated tremendous euphoria and optimism. The new spirit of the times was hostile to realism, which is a dour and pessimistic doctrine, one that stresses the inevitability of conflict, the intractability of interests, the dangers of life in a world of sovereign States. The virtues it most strongly recommends are prudence and vigilance. No one caught the new spirit better than Francis Fukuyama, whose book, *The End of History and the Last Man* – destined to be translated into twenty-two languages – devoted two whole chapters to an attack on realism.

Liberals in particular were in the mood to dismiss realism, having spent most of the Cold War either in futile opposition to, or very reluctant support for, a realist policy that was temperamentally uncongenial to them. Realism is an affront to liberalism in many ways. It stresses conflict as a central and enduring fact of life; liberalism asserts the true and peaceful harmony of interests, obscured only by temporary and removable ignorance and misunderstanding. Classic realists like Reinhold Niebuhr and Hans Morgenthau postulate a universal and unchanging human nature, one that is incorrigibly selfish and power-seeking, as the root of international conflict; liberals believe either in the innate goodness of man, or in a malleable human nature that can be made good by wise policy and a suitable environment.

Again, liberals believe profoundly in the redeeming power of institutions – the League of Nations, the United Nations, the European Union, or whatever – to change, to transform reality. Like the celestial voice urging the man to build a baseball stadium in that bad movie, *Field of Dreams*, they have a sort of 'Build it and they will come' approach to the relationships between structures and behaviour. Realists on the other hand believe that institutions essentially reflect reality and have a very limited capacity to change it.

The liberal rejection of realism since the end of the Cold War has come in various forms, most of them representing very durable ideas and powerful longings that have survived repeated disappointments. As Frank Johnson has nicely observed, 'In politics, Utopia is always an important country, always one of the Great Powers.' And the Polish satirist Stanislaw Lec sardonically advises, 'When smashing the monuments, save the pedestals. They always come in handy.'

The most superficial utopian, anti-realist line has been Salvation through the United Nations, now free for the first time to function as it was supposed to. A short but adequate response to this is that if the United Nations is the answer, the question is wrongly framed. The United Nations does not replace power politics, it merely disguises it and increases its hypocrisy content. As that old Australian realist, Robert Menzies, once said of faith in the United Nations, believing that it can transform international politics is like believing in the possibility of erecting a house which will then be capable of digging its own foundations.

A much more interesting version of post-Cold War optimism and one that challenges realism more seriously is the Salvation through Democracy thesis: Democracy is spreading rapidly and the historical record shows that democracies do not go to war with each other; therefore we are moving to a state of affairs in which war will become obsolete.

Now we can quibble endlessly about the record and the details, but the historical claim is in fact pretty sound (at least, if you agree that Germany was not a democracy in 1914). This leaves us with a crucial question: whether what has been substantially true up to now of a very limited number of democracies, overwhelmingly Western in culture and Christian in religion, will remain true of a much larger and culturally diverse number of democracies in the future. That is, has it been the political system or the culture that has been the crucial factor in determining the behaviour of Western democracies towards each other? I do not know the answer to that question, and neither, I believe, do those who argue the democratic case. But this is one of the many forms in which the question of culture is increasingly intruding itself into international politics.

That apart, the democratic argument serves to draw attention to one of the most serious shortcomings of realism, which is this: In its stress on the structure of the international system – that is, on the state of anarchy among sovereign States – realism attaches little or no importance to what is going on *inside* particular States – what kind of regimes are in power, what kind of ideologies prevail, what kind of leadership is provided. According to realists, and especially the so-called neo-realists, the foreign policies of all States, regardless of differences in their political makeup, are basically driven by the same systemic factors. As the much used analogy has it, they are like so many billiard balls, obeying the same laws of political geometry and physics.

Now all this is enormously counter-intuitive and a real weakness, especially in an age of ideology. Did it really make no difference to German foreign policy whether the regime in power was the Weimar Republic or the Nazi dictatorship? Was it not precisely the failure to recognize the difference that led Neville Chamberlain to the fatally mistaken belief that he could cut a deal with – appease – Hitler in the traditional way?

It might seem that such questions are purely rhetorical and that just to pose them is to answer them. But that is not so. That there was continuity in German foreign policy – that the policy of Hitler was essentially no different from that of Stresemann and Brüning – was, after all, the central assumption of A. J. P. Taylor's best-selling book *The Origins of the Second World War*. That continuity was also assumed in E. H. Carr's enormously influential realist treatise, *The Twenty Years' Crisis*, appropriately described by Taylor as 'a brilliant argument in favour of appeasement'. Cold War realists brought off the neat trick of presenting the appeasement policies of the 1930s as entirely the product of the illusions associated with soft liberal internationalism, but that is self-serving. The Oxford Union and the editor of the *New Statesman* did not govern Britain. Appeasement was directly the product of the limited understanding resulting from the shallow realism of Tory politicians and Foreign Office officials, a realism that was ill-equipped to understand the terrible novelty of Nazi totalitarianism. As a standard work on the subject points out, 'For the appeasers it was the height of "realism" to criticize the Versailles Treaty . . . [and] it was "practical politics" to advocate Treaty revisions in Germany's favour'.*

I emphasize this weakness of realism – its comparative insensitivity and indifference towards changes in the internal political makeup of countries – because, as I shall discuss later, I believe it is very evident and important today.**

A third challenge to realism in the post-Cold War era is even more fundamental and strikes at the basic premise of the realist approach. The political world is, according to realists, chopped up vertically into sovereign States. These States have boundaries that they control and defend and regard as inviolable. International politics is about relations between these vertically divided States.

Until now that has obviously been a basically true picture of the

* Gilbert and Gott, *The Appeasers*, Weidenfeld and Nicolson, 1963, pp. 5–6.

** As well as its shallowness, another feature of this kind of realism is its passive, deterministic character. It tends to take everything into account except the potential force of one's own will, thus leaving one immobilized. It is the realism of decline and failing confidence.

political world. No longer, say an increasing number of influential voices, who claim that this vertical version of the world is rapidly being replaced by a horizontally ordered one. The decisive forces in today's world – and even more so in tomorrow's world – it is asserted, are capital, technology and, especially, information. Increasingly, and with ever greater velocity, these spread horizontally across the surface of the earth, recognizing no impediments, no national limits. We are moving rapidly towards a borderless world in which sovereignty is a myth, the State a fiction, and interdependence and integration the overriding realities. In such a world, State rivalries and military force make little sense – the realist's world is an anachronism.

This, essentially, is the sermon preached by many leaders of industry, as well as by academics and intellectuals. You could hear a forceful version of it, for example, in Rupert Murdoch's recent Bonython lecture, delivered in Melbourne, and he himself embodies much of what this world view is about.

What can one say about it? A lot, but I'll just make four points. First, while it presents itself as a cutting-edge view, it has a very familiar ring to it. A century and a half ago, Marx and Engels were declaring that in place of the old local and national seclusion and self-sufficiency, there was 'interaction in every direction, universal interdependence of nations', and going on to announce the withering away of States, as a result. Well, they have been a long time withering and have shown themselves to be extremely tough, durable and adaptable institutions.

Second, it makes the very naive assumption that propinquity automatically produces greater harmony and has no downside. The fact that most murders still happen in the family should be enough to indicate the dubious quality of that assumption. An example of the assumption in action was provided in Rupert Murdoch's speech, in which he celebrated the fact that technology was ending the 'tyranny of distance' over Australian life; there was no recognition that also ending was the *shield* of distance, hitherto Australia's greatest strategic asset.

Third, according to some economic historians, the degree of interdependence now is no greater, perhaps not as great, as it was at the beginning of this century in Europe, when capital was moving freely, there was mass migration of labour, and trade as a proportion of global production was higher than it is now. All that had little effect on the course of power politics.

Fourth, this picture of the world is very Western-centric. If the United States and European countries have allowed their borders to become very porous in many respects, this is certainly *not* true of much of the rest of the world – not of Japan or China or Iran, or Korea, for instance. Henry Kissinger recently observed that there is little Wilsonian idealism in Asia; and, he could have added, neither is there much 'borderless worldism'.

As for the West itself, it might be claimed that the European Union is clear evidence that horizontal forces are triumphing, vertical barriers are disappearing, and a new community is emerging. That is certainly how enthusiasts present the matter. But when such a process is restricted to a region, it represents not a threat to the system but a rearrangement of power within it – as happened, say, in nineteenth-century Germany and Italy. If it continues, its outcome will not be the end of the state system but the emergence of a new superpower, in the form of a German-dominated Europe.

Utopianism is the most obvious and familiar of realism's adversaries, but it is not the only one. In so far as realism's first commitment is to try to see things as they are, without illusion or distortion, another of its enemies is habit – that is, the inclination to see things as they *were*. This is a more insidious adversary, since realism's assumption of continuity is conducive and congenial to habit. And while, after forty-five years of Cold War, there was a conscious reaction against it, there has also been an unconscious, unexamined carrying over of many of its habits of thought and behaviour to the new era.

Let us look at the two erstwhile superpowers in these terms. The immediate and natural reaction to the end of the Cold War was that the collapse of one superpower left the other supreme. The United States as 'the sole remaining superpower' would dominate the scene and its will would shape the new era. As cool a customer as Richard Nixon declared extravagantly that 'because we are the last remaining superpower, no crisis is irrelevant to our interests'. American leadership in the Gulf War initially seemed to confirm this view (especially if one overlooked the fact that subsequently the United States had to take around the hat to ask for donations to finance the venture).

True, since then the United States has been much more indecisive and ineffectual, but most commentators have been content to blame that on the incompetence of the Clinton administration, an accidental and temporary factor whose importance can be played down.

I have argued elsewhere that such an explanation is inadequate and superficial; that, for deeper reasons, the United States is unlikely to perform effectively the role thus designated to it. Recent fiascos reflect not only the indisputable incompetence of the Clinton administration but a tension between old Cold War habits and new inhibitions and preoccupations.*

The phrase 'sole remaining superpower' is an oxymoron, a contradiction in terms, at least when applied to a country like the United States. The superpower game is a relational one, not solitaire. If you have two superpowers and you take one away, what you have left is less than a superpower – because the incentive, the compulsion to mobilize and deploy resources, to convert potential into performance is no longer there. In the case of cancerous States like Napoleonic France, Hitler's Germany or Stalin's Soviet Union, the motivation for dominance can be self-generated and insatiable. In normal states it cannot – it needs the galvanizing sense of danger and threat that the presence of a great rival creates. Capacity, potential: these alone do not make a superpower, otherwise the United States would have been a superpower back in the 1920s, which, of course, it wasn't.

In the case of the United States, a very activist foreign policy needs a great goal to drive it. Hence the obsession with formulating 'doctrines' and the current demand for ennobling 'visions'. Such a great defining goal is now lacking. In its absence, America will not dominate and stamp its will, and gradually new priorities and inhibitions will affect its pattern of behaviour, setting narrower limits: the need to attend to pressing domestic matters; the reluctance to take casualties except when vital interests are concerned; the need for multilateral cover to justify its actions. A superpower is, by definition, one that is given vast resources, power and freedom of action; but the current trend in American politics – supported both by Congress and the President – is to limit and reduce the powers of the

* Owen Harries, 'My So-Called Foreign Policy', *The New Republic*, 10 October, 1994, p. 24.

central government, to divert more resources and authority to the states. In a recent interview, Newt Gingrich, who more than any other single person set the agenda for the new Congress after the November 1994 election, said that he was too preoccupied with domestic affairs to give foreign policy any consideration in 1995. He went on to explain that while he was a hawk, he was a 'cheap hawk' who wanted to cut the defence budget. At the same time, however, the Republican victory represented a decisive repudiation of multilateralism in foreign policy, the only way to get activism on the cheap.

Turning to the other erstwhile superpower, Russia, I believe that this is a case in which the shortcomings and dangers of the realist approach are clearly evident. To say again, realism deals in States, not regimes, and maintains that the foreign policies of States tend to be continuous over long periods, regardless of regime changes. It is not surprising, then, that leading realists, notably Kissinger and Brzezinski, tend to view Russia today with very much the same suspicion and wariness – if not hostility – that they showed towards the Soviet Union. Their expectations of imperialist behaviour are largely shaped by the history of Soviet and, before that, Tsarist foreign policy, and there is little inclination to give any benefit of the doubt to the struggling democratic government in Moscow.

Again, questions arise: What were we opposing in the Cold War – a totalitarian regime and ideology, or Russia as Russia? Was not a democratic Russia one of the outcomes we *sought* – not only because it would be better for the Russians, but because it would make it an easier country to live with? If so, instead of presuming a continuation of bad behaviour, and basing policy accordingly (notably by the incredibly provocative eastward expansion of NATO), should we not be prepared to exercise some patience and remember Churchill's advice: in victory, magnanimity (especially as the country in question still possesses an enormous arsenal of nuclear weapons)? Are there not distinctions to be made between imperialist behaviour and a desperate attempt to hold a chaotic country together? And, regrettable as it is, is it not virtually inevitable that a period of great transition will be characterized by some violence and brutality? (Think of the British departure from India or Kenya; or the French from Vietnam or Algeria.)

These are vitally important questions. Once already in this century,

Western countries created a terrible crisis and allowed an unnecessary world war to happen because they assumed that the foreign policy of a totalitarian regime would be no different from that of the struggling democracy it replaced. It would be inexcusable and disastrous if they made the same error in reverse at the end of the century, proceeding as if the behaviour of a nascent democracy will be no different from the totalitarian Soviet regime that preceded it. The great danger with Russia today is not imperialism, but anarchy and chaos – not an assertive, purposeful State, but the collapse of the State. And to the extent that it has energy to spare for foreign policy in the next decades, events are more likely to direct its attention to the East and the South – to its borders with China and Islam – than to the West.

I've mentioned NATO, so let me turn to that question. Here again, habit is the problem, combined with powerful vested interests. NATO was a magnificent Cold War achievement, arguably the most successful alliance in history. But the threat it was meant to contain, the force it was meant to balance, no longer exist. Yet the survival – and indeed the expansion – of NATO is treated as a vital issue; and the continuing political and strategic unity of 'the West' is taken for granted as a permanent fact of life, though except during the periods of hot and cold world wars of this century it has never existed before.

There are, of course, powerful vested interests involved here, many careers and contracts and consultancies and reputations. But the most powerful vested interest involved is in certain ideas and ways of looking at things with which we are comfortable: in yesterday's realism. As Lord Salisbury once said, 'The commonest error in politics is sticking to the carcass of dead policies.' And as Walter Wriston recently observed of the World Bank, 'When an organization's mission has been completed and its presence no longer required, there are almost no instances of simply liquidating it, turning its lights out and going home. Instead a new mission is invented, since the real objective of bureaucracies – public or private – is survival.'

It is not a matter of advocating the immediate abolition of NATO. Abrupt discontinuities usually create more problems than they solve. But allowing the preserving of an old institution, one whose ostensible purpose has disappeared, to dictate policy – and that is what is explicitly advocated in such NATO slogans as 'expand or perish' and 'out of area or out of business' – is dangerous. It is especially dangerous when no one has the slightest intention of honouring the new obligations that would be involved in expansion; and does anyone seriously believe that any Western country would (could) take significant casualties in defence of, say, Slovakia or Hungary?

A further striking example of the grip of habit is that people continue speaking of 'the West' while simultaneously advancing the incompatible opinion that the structure of the new era will be triangular or tripolar, with North America, Asia–Pacific and Europe representing the three poles. Such a tripolar conceptualization, of course, denies the unity of the West and splits it up into two separate, competing parts, but still the term is used as a politically meaningful one.

Speaking of the tripolar model brings the Asia–Pacific region into the picture, and this raises a different, and very intriguing kind of question. The realist theory of foreign policy was developed on the basis of the experience of Western States, and indeed for several centuries all the principal actors in world politics, all the great powers, belonged to that one civilization. Power politics was a Western game, so cultural or civilizational factors did not come into consideration because they were a constant. The first significant partial exception to this was Japan in the middle of this century, and its attitude towards diplomacy, war, the treatment of prisoners and so on suggested that all Western generalizations might not hold true for other cultures. Ruth Benedict's famous work, *The Chrysanthemum and the Sword*, was an early attempt to probe this question. Then, three decades ago, a serious American misreading of the political culture of Vietnam prepared the way for the greatest political and military humiliations in the modern history of the United States.

Now, with the political and economic rise of States in other civilizations – particularly in Asia – the question has become urgent. Will the generalizations of realism apply and hold true for non-Western actors who are destined to assume a much greater role in the scheme of things? Will the universal human nature that classical realism posits, or the international anarchy that neo-realism sees as crucial, override the cultural differences between civilizations?

Some raised early doubts in this respect. As long ago as 1968, for example, the International Institute of Strategic Studies published a paper by Coral Bell arguing that the central realist notion of a balance of power system was foreign to China, with that country's traditional belief that 'there can only be one sun in the sky', and its model of a kind of solar system of imperial dependencies and vassal States around the sun of the Middle Kingdom.* But other China specialists, notably John Fairbanks of Harvard, disputed such a view, speaking of the 'deeply ingrained attitude towards foreign relations as a problem in the balancing of foreign powers against each other to China's advantage'.** Certainly, Henry Kissinger, no mean judge, has been very impressed with the Chinese grasp of *Realpolitik*. But as against this, for long periods of the Cold War, China simultaneously alienated both superpowers, showing no concern for balancing one against the other.

Again, some would argue that the fact that Japan in recent years has become the second most powerful economic power in the world without developing comparable military power and without engaging seriously in great power politics shows that it is different in kind. But, of course, Japan has behaved in this way while its security was being looked after by a friendly and dominant United States – in very much the same way that the United States itself, in an earlier age, did not engage very actively in power politics as long as its interests were protected by a friendly British Navy. That is, it might not have a cultural explanation but a political and strategic one, and it might not outlive the favourable condition of American protection and American maintenance of an Asia–Pacific balance.

Because of the Japanese example and the incredible economic strides being made in the region, there is some temptation to assume that, in the Asia–Pacific region more than anywhere else, economic power will replace military power as the principal currency of international politics. Perhaps; but we should be very careful about depending on it. An awful lot of people have died violent death in the Asia–Pacific region in this century, and there seems to be little ground for assuming that the accumulation and use of military force will be uncongenial, if it can be done to advantage. Certainly the

* Coral Bell, 'The Asian Balance of Power: A Comparison with European Precedents', Adelphi Papers No. 44, (I.I.S.S., London, 1968).

** John Fairbanks, *The US and China*, (Harvard, U.P., 1958) p. 305.

main principled (as opposed to prudential) constraint on the resort to force in the West – the liberal conscience – does not appear to be a prominent characteristic of Asian cultures.

Some argue that as economic growth proceeds and 'modernization' occurs, the question of cultural differences and their consequences will become insignificant. Asia will become more like us, usually meaning more liberal and democratic. Again, perhaps, though many of the smartest Asians insist that in their case there will be a different synthesis of economic, social and political elements. Whether this is true or not – whether there is only one modernizing road, the Western one, or several – seems to me one of the crucial questions of our time. In a recent issue of *The National Interest*, a Western academic at the University of Singapore, David Martin Jones, argues that those who believe that the rising middle classes in Asia will perform the same political functions as they did earlier in the West – that is, pressing for democracy, a civil society and human rights – are doomed to be disappointed, that these Asian middle classes are regime-supporting and stability-oriented. I'm not sure whether he will be promoted, demoted, deported, or caned for saying this.*

I have emphasized the extent to which realism can be an effective antidote both to the wishful fantasies of Utopians and to the grip of habit. Its sobriety and coolness is also the best antidote to the doom-laden and rather hysterical prophecies of distopians, or black utopians, those who see the world as rapidly and unstoppably going to hell. I make the point because, after the initial grand hopes that accompanied the end of the Cold War cooled or were disappointed – after Bosnia and Somalia and Rwanda and Georgia and Chechnya – there has recently been a pronounced swing to doom-saying. Fashionable American intellectuals are now talking of 'chaos theory'. A great deal of attention was given not long ago, for example, to an article by Robert Kaplan titled 'The Coming Anarchy' that appeared in the *Atlantic Monthly*,** an article now destined to be expanded into a book.

In my opinion Kaplan's is a very poor article, sensational and

* David Martin Jones, 'Asia's New Middle Class,' *The National Interest* No. 38, Winter 1994–5. The author has since left Singapore to teach in Tasmania.
** *The Atlantic Monthly*, February 1994.

unargued, the sort of thing that gives pessimism a bad name. Its commitment to a catastrophic view of the future is such that it offers, without any serious argument, contemporary West Africa as a paradigm of the world's future, a world of gross overpopulation, environmental degradation, crime, corruption, and a general breakdown of government and civil society. While he is eloquent on the horrors of West Africa, the success story of East Asia is hardly mentioned.

Some of the problems and dangers that are pointed to are, of course, real and serious enough. But like their utopian opposites, what the distopians do is to focus on a few trends, treat them as irreversible, ignore countervailing forces, allow for no surprises, and for no learning and corrective action. Realism is a good counter to distopianism both because its natural, controlled pessimism acts as an inoculation against extreme kinds of panic-mongering, and because its commitment to trying to see things as they are involves a balanced appraisal, taking into account positive factors as well as negative ones.

A disposition to see things as they are, without distortion or illusion – that, and that alone, constitutes the essence of realism. Everything else about it, its positive content as an intellectual position or doctrine, is in principle negotiable and dispensable, as the world changes. In practice, of course, things are different. Investments in and commitments to particular tenets of the realist position, as formulated in the schools, cause intellectual rigidities and become impediments to seeing things as they are and how they are changing.

What Elie Kedourie once said of conservative discourse – that it is the one which 'hugs most closely the shape of this world' – is also true of realist discourse. That is its strength but also its limitation: admirable in describing the 'shape' of an existing state of affairs, it can give little account of movement and innovation. Realism has no theory of change, is resistant to the possibility of novelty. In the past this has not mattered much because it has been dealing with the consequences of a central fact – the primacy of sovereign States, Western sovereign States, in international affairs – which has been remarkably constant.

The question now is whether that central fact is changing in ways that require a serious reformulation of realism. It seems to me that the two most far-reaching problems for realism today are those posed by 'horizontal' forces, and by the rising significance of non-Western countries, particularly in the Asia–Pacific region and the Islamic world. As to the former, I express some scepticism based on a past experience of false alarms, though, of course, the fact that pronouncements have been wrong in the past is not conclusive. Almost certainly *some* important consequences for international politics are going to flow from the extraordinary revolution in communication, and realists should be pondering what they may be rather than simply sitting pat and putting their faith in the durability of the sovereign state.

As for the coming multicultural character of international politics, the nature of the consequent interaction between civilizational factors on the one hand and state interests and power on the other is emerging as perhaps the most intriguing question of our time. Samuel Huntington, a man of realist disposition and the most fertile mind in American political science in recent decades, has already taken a bold – perhaps over-bold – shot at addressing it. Other realists should follow his example. They might do worse than begin by considering whether the experience of the Cold War – when traditional notions of national interests were to some extent displaced by the solidarist claims made in the name of those grander entities, 'the West' and 'the Free World' – to some extent and in some ways prefigured the way things are going to be in the age of multicultural power politics.

In times of great change, realism requires not only an insistence on the importance of what remains the same (though it certainly requires that, and though that has been realism's distinctive contribution until now) but a serious and imaginative effort to understand the significance of what is new.

Whatever the future of realism as an intellectual *position*, it is certain to remain the most appropriate *disposition* with which to approach international politics. Having started by quoting the Great Whig, let me end by quoting a comment by the Great Tory that seems to me to encapsulate in vivid form the essence of that disposition.

In the midst of an argument about the most appropriate way of dealing with an obstreperous person, Dr Johnson once delivered himself of this:

> If a madman were to come into this room with a stick in his hand, no doubt we should pity the state of his mind; but our

> primary consideration would be to take care of ourselves. We should knock him down first, and pity him afterwards.

There you have most of what is central to the realist disposition: its awareness of danger as a natural part of life; its stress on self-reliance and its guiltless acknowledgement of the need to put self-interest first; its willingness to use force prudentially; the priority that is necessarily given to survival; and the consequent recognition that while humanitarian impulses are fine, they cannot be overriding.

Nothing is likely to happen anytime soon that will render any of this irrelevant or invalid.

X

THREE CONSERVATIVE REALISTS

KENNETH MINOGUE

'Theory has become the opium of the masses.'

ELIE KEDOURIE*

Michael Oakeshott, Shirley Letwin and Elie Kedourie were three conservative thinkers who also happened to have been great friends. Oakeshott and Kedourie both taught at the London School of Economics. Shirley Letwin taught there only for a short time, but was always closely associated with the School. Hence one way we might name them is as the 'LSE conservatives'. They also shared the fatality of dying within three years of each other. They often met, sometimes at LSE, sometimes at intellectual parties in London, perhaps most intimately at the Letwin drawing room in Kent Terrace by Regents Park. Each of them wrote for an overlapping range of publications, which included outlets as various as the *Cambridge Review*, *Encounter*, *Times Literary Supplement* and the *Daily Telegraph*, as well as academic journals.

My argument is that they constituted the core of an intellectual school or movement which was both conservative and philosophical. It is true, indeed, that Oakeshott, the oldest and the originating philosophical figure, regarded the expression 'conservative philosopher' as a category mistake, but like any philosopher, he will have to put up with a good deal of posthumous vulgarization, and I hope that vital distinctions underlying this sensibility will soon emerge. But our first task must be to locate these people on a broader intellectual map.

Each of them supported much that was done by Margaret Thatcher's government after 1979. They certainly rejected commu-

* Elie Kedourie, *Nationalism in Asia and Africa*, New York: World Publishing, 1970, p. 147.

nism and all forms of totalitarianism, in the spirit of those who supported the 'free world' after 1945. More specifically, they agreed with much of the classical liberal or libertarian criticism of social democracy advanced by Hayek and Friedman. Shirley Letwin, in particular, was a great friend of both, and like her husband William Letwin, was a *habitué* of the Institute of Economic Affairs. Oakeshott remained largely remote from what he called, with some derision, 'the world', but both Letwin and Kedourie wrote for the Centre for Policy Studies. To this familiar world, then, they belonged, but what concerns me is what distinguished them from it.

The high tide of classical liberal ideas and their notable triumph over communism during the 1980s has been followed by an undertow advancing the values of community against what (in the crudest formulation) is described as 'excessive' individualism. The adjective here suggests an idea of a person as merely a bundle of impulses, and carries with it the further suggestion that impulses are all right in moderation, but that the moral bounds must be set not by the legal entity of the State, but by the social, or perhaps moral entity of the community. The relation between the individual and the State is by this transformation of our inherited conception of individuality switched away from the rule of law towards the polarities of selfishness and altruism. The moralizing of impulses essential to real individualism is thus invested in what is vaguely called 'the community'. In their different ways, Etzioni in America and John Gray in Britain have been vehicles of this new fashion for taking moral and political bearings from the community. What distinguishes the conservatism of the group I am describing is that it transcends this fashion by bringing out what is involved in liberal democratic association.

To identify these scholars as conservative might simply mean that they were sympathetic to the policies of the British Conservative Party, and sometimes they were. Much more important, however, is their view that the activity of conserving an *established* way of life is the central, indeed virtually the defining, concern of politics. This is the sense in which most practising politicians, whatever their party affiliation, have always been in large degree conservative. In earlier times, as Hugh Cecil once wrote,* conservatism was barely visible

* Hugh Cecil, *Conservatism*, London, 1912, p. 25.

because there was little else. In modern politics, however, the power of the State has so increased as to induce the bewitching dream of perfecting the human race from the top. To every evil, it seems, there must be a legislative remedy: hence the coming of what one might call 'the politics of the big idea'. Adhesion to some such project of revolution or reform is what most centrally we mean by the term 'liberalism'. In its generic sense, liberalism stands for what most distinguishes *modern* politics from the politics of earlier centuries. Our century has become a laboratory for ideas, both big, and bigger. Totalitarian versions of class or racial community, as advanced by Nazism and communism, were the melodramatic cases; welfarism has been the typical big idea of liberal democracies. The failure of totalitarianism, and the rising costs (both moral and financial) of welfare have, for the moment at least, taught most people the conservative virtue of moderation. Conservatives are no longer regarded as eccentric survivals of less enlightened times. The price for this new acceptance, however, is that it is much more difficult to know quite what it is to be a conservative. Most traditional moral resources have now become so extensively submerged in perfectionist projects that in trying to decide what to conserve, or even what to restore, conservatives have to some degree fallen into the same predicament as their opponents: they must make some rational selection among policies to be presented to democratic electorates as the next 'big idea'. The formulation of a conservative attitude is much more difficult because when *everything* has the form of a project, it is difficult to discover which policies sustain the inherited fabric of life, and which are mere expressions of reforming restlessness. And the sheer semantic problem has been dramatized by the practice of referring to old-guard communists in Eastern Europe as 'conservative'.

An obvious conservative move amid such an intellectual tempest would be to ground conservatism in religious or metaphysical certainty. None of the LSE conservatives opted for this possibility. All of them have indeed been sympathetic to religion but they have not sought to build political conclusions upon it. Nor have they had recourse to philosophical foundations, such as Natural Law. In this respect, they are curiously similar to the postmodernist sceptics who are currently the most destructive bulls in the china shop of the West. This is no doubt one of the reasons why our three conservatives are regarded with some suspicion by American neo-conservatives. The most celebrated among the postmodernist philosophers, Richard Rorty, has even claimed Oakeshott (and especially Oakeshott's conception of a culture as a conversation) as part of his own heritage.

The scepticism and relativism of modern intellectuality in our time has been characterized in the Cole Porter formula as 'anything goes'. Our three writers were very far from singing this song. They were all marked by a deep respect for historical tradition. They built political understanding, as we all must, out of the actual moral and cultural character they themselves enjoyed, and especially for Kedourie and Letwin, that identity was a chosen one. Shirley Letwin and Elie Kedourie were both Jewish, the one from Chicago, the other from Iraq. Both of them came to Britain to study, and not only stayed but embraced a British sense of politics. When Shirley Letwin traced one development in British political ideas through the stages of a belief in certainty, evolving through the ideas of Hume, Bentham, Mill and Beatrice Webb, she was clear that 'the change that can be traced through their lives is a story of a departure from, a decline of, a uniquely British pattern'.*

Michael Oakeshott, by contrast, had been born a generation earlier, and was English to his fingertips. Many of his loyalties and attitudes were recognizably Edwardian, a period marked in many areas by a self-conscious Britishness. Irony and distance were of his essence, and he had a deep distrust of the pretentious. A small example: in a review of T. D. Weldon's *The Vocabulary of Politics*, he began:

> This is a light-hearted book, and is all the better for being so: philosophy is getting rid of one's phlegm, and this should not be a very solemn exercise. Mr Weldon may make things look a little easier than they are, but he is mainly concerned with removing spurious difficulties, which is always a grateful task.**

In his famous preoccupation with conversation, Oakeshott was certainly thinking of the saloon bar rather than the salon or the common room. A gentleness of manner belied an almost stoical toughness.

* Shirley Letwin, *The Pursuit of Certainty*, Cambridge: Cambridge University Press, 1965, p. 3.

** Michael Oakeshott, 'A Question of Politics', *Spectator*, 9 October 1953.

Neither nature nor culture, he was clear, guarantee the human world we cherish, and to look for security was not to live in any world he was familiar with. Living dangerously was not something to be embraced with Nietzschean exhilaration; given the universe we inhabit, it was merely a fate to be accepted.

Conservatism in this philosophy was something carefully circumscribed. For Oakeshott, it was merely one disposition among others, while Letwin, attempting to understand 'Thatcherism', was emphatic that its precepts responded merely to that time and to this place. Their emphasis on historical identity might well associate them with Burke, but they never made much of him. Kedourie seems to have picked up the Namierite view of Burke as a rather dodgy adventurer, while Oakeshott, skirting close to construing conservatism in terms of tradition during the period he wrote about rationalism, soon moved to the more abstract questions which issued in his analysis of the different types of human association in *On Human Conduct*. He took issue with Russell Kirk's view that Burke initiated 'the canons of modern conservatism' on the ground that 'the *disposition* [my italics] they represented had already been fully revealed in seventeenth-century England, and Burke's thoughts were composed of an appropriate selection of long-current and well-tried notions'. Burke and Oakeshott had contrasting temperaments, and Oakeshott thought that 'on account of his speculative moderation and his clear recognition of politics as a specific activity, it would perhaps have been more fortunate if the modern conservative had paid more attention to Hume and less to Burke'.* I have italicized the word 'disposition' in the quotation above because here, and in his better known essay on conservatism in *Rationalism in Politics*, Oakeshott keeps clear of doctrine and prefers to treat conservatism as merely one disposition culturally on offer in the Western political tradition (and hence not

* Michael Oakeshott, 'Conservative Political Thought', *Spectator*, 15 October 1954. In view of the theme of Conor Cruise O'Brien's recent book on Burke entitled *The Great Melody, A Thematic Biography of Edmund Burke*, University of Chicago Press, 1992, it is interesting to note that Oakeshott went on to say: 'Burke was not, indeed, a great composer at all; he was something much rarer, a great intellectual melodist whose tunes were all the sweeter because they owed so much to the intellectual folk-music of Europe. Others, coming after him, produced grandiose compositions, but what these owed to Burke was not their architectonic but whatever melodiousness they managed to retain.'

grounded in any such natural characteristic as age). He was also clear that one might be disposed to be conservative in politics, and adventurous and risk-taking in everything else. Just such a contrast, as it happens, characterized Britain in the eighteenth and nineteenth centuries. (The tragedy of Russia in our century, it might be remarked, is that it has been radical and adventurous in its politics, and in nothing else.)

Englishness (rather than the more abstract and political Britishness) was at the centre of Oakeshott's sensibilities, as it also was for Letwin, who formulated what she found most striking in this tradition as the idea of the gentleman. Kedourie shared the same concrete sense of Englishness, but was preoccupied with the theme of its decadence, which he dated from the late nineteenth century and identified, in the first place, with a sense of imperial guilt that had spread through the educated classes.

Oakeshott is sometimes criticized as someone who had no sense of the brutal realities of power. This was not a charge that could be levelled at Kedourie. His account of both nationalism and the history of Middle Eastern politics clearly recognizes both the centrality of power and the contingency of its operation. He commented, for example, that Fichte's theory of the State as the creator of man's internal and spiritual freedom 'tends to disguise the element of violence that accompanies all government'. Applied to the real world (he went on) such a phraseology would 'hide under soft euphemisms the hard issues of power, which, by its very nature, is exercised by some over others ... to clothe issues of power in religious or aesthetic terminology can lead to a misleading and dangerous confusion.'* Later in *Nationalism* he remarked that the best that can be said is that nationalism is an attempt to establish once and for all the reign of justice in a corrupt world. 'But this best is bad enough, since to repair such injuries other injuries must in turn be inflicted, and no balance is ever struck in the grisly account of cruelty and violence.'** Scepticism about grand plans of perfecting this human condition was central to Kedourie's thought. In his conversation, scepticism about political outcomes in general would commonly be expressed in a

* Elie Kedourie, *Nationalism*, London: Hutchinson, 1960, pp. 47–8.
** *Ibid*, p. 139.

characteristic shrug, as Kedourie would ask: 'How can one know?' He was also acutely aware that high ideals and low motives often go together.

For each of these thinkers, conservatism was a belief about the touchstone of reality, and it was a form of reality central to their thought precisely because they did not believe in solid moral and political foundations. The grim consequences of detachment from reality appeared in many guises, and perhaps most strikingly in three episodes central to British (and more broadly to Anglo-Saxon) experience in the twentieth century. The first was the problem of dealing with the threat of Nazism, encapsulated in the idea of 'appeasement'. The second was the welfare state created by the Attlee government of 1945, an episode of a type repeated in President Johnson's 'war against poverty' after 1964. The third was the youth movement of the 1960s which thought to repeal the law of original sin.

Only Oakeshott was of an age to respond directly to the crisis of the 1930s and he seems to have taken little intellectual cognizance of it as a practical question. When war came, however, he joined the army and served in a notably risky unit called 'Phantom'. His response to the welfare state was vastly more articulate. It took the form of analysing and attacking the broad intellectual movement he called 'rationalism'. This was Oakeshott's account of the complex thing that appears in other political philosophies as the Straussian 'modernity' or the 'Enlightenment project' of the Frankfurt School, or Heidegger's technology or Voegelin's gnosticism. These ideas are philosophy's contribution to the self-understanding of the modern age.

In his treatment of rationalism during the late 1940s, Oakeshott came close to taking up an actual political position. But even in treating of contemporary politics under the rubric of rationalism, he was philosophical enough to transpose his polemic out of immediate practicalities and into a concern with an erroneous epistemology: Rationalism was the belief that the conditions of any activity could be exhaustively formulated in precepts. It was not, however, merely a false belief. It was nothing less than a corruption of the mind.* It suffered from the defect of being systematically unable to correct its

* Michael Oakeshott, *Rationalism in Politics and Other Essays*, foreword by Timothy Fuller, Indianapolis: Liberty Press, 1991, p. 37.

own shortcomings. The rationalist 'does not merely neglect the kind of knowledge which would save him, he begins by destroying it. First he turns out the light and then complains that he cannot see . . . All the rationalist can do when left to himself is to replace one rationalist project in which he has failed by another in which he hopes to succeed.' In practical terms, then, Oakeshott is deeply pessimistic. A rationalist culture is beyond the reach of self-help, and the flounderings of political parties merely illustrate the predicament. The common response to Oakeshott's criticism of rationalism was the rationalist complaint that he failed to offer us guidance about what we must do in order to be saved!

The framework within which this account of contemporary politics (and much else) was located is a view of the human condition. Like any conservative, Oakeshott rejected the liberal conception of progressive human improvement. He was on the one hand enchanted by the prodigies of imagination revealed in human art and history, and on the other recognized that mankind is 'a race condemned to seek its perfection in the flying moment and always in the one to come, [and] whose highest virtue must be to cultivate a clear-sighted vision of the consequences of its actions'. Its 'greatest need (not supplied by nature) is freedom from the distraction of illusion'.* Rationalism is the paradigm form of illusion in our time. The world is overrun with sorcerer's apprentices and (if I may mix Oakeshott's myths) the modern project is to build a tower of Babel – to seek 'perfection as the crow flies' was the way Oakeshott put it.

These reflections come, as it were, from Oakeshott's middle period, when his view of the modern world became visible in the interstices of his philosophical preoccupations, but the central point to understand about Oakeshott is simply that he was a philosopher, though one who understood all too well the attractions of what he called, in *Experience and its Modes*, the 'empty kisses of abstraction' within whose embrace human life must be lived. Philosophy, by contrast with the unmeditated delights of practical satisfaction, is an austere, almost perverse, occupation for a human being. When Oakeshott wrote about conservatism as a disposition, he refined it to a philosophical

* Thomas Hobbes, *Leviathan*, edited by Michael Oakeshott, Oxford: Basil Blackwell, p. lxvi.

universal such as could not possibly be found pure in the actual world. Again, when he sought to understand the State, he analysed it into forms of association, and what is unique in the institution of the State is to be found in what he calls *civil* association. Where, however, can one find a set of real, living human beings merely enjoying the 'watery fidelity' of civil association without also being involved in at least the shadow of a common enterprise? The point is that philosophy is not description, and the reality of the philosopher is only one of the many kinds of lucidity needed in human life. Indeed, in his most austere moments, Oakeshott doubted whether philosophical understanding was valuable in practice at all.

Kedourie, by contrast, was very directly concerned with political reality. He resembled Joseph Conrad in being a master stylist in English in spite of, or perhaps because of, the fact that English was not the first exercise for his tongue. He occasionally used slang, or unusual words, with gleeful relish. Who else, for example, would have characterized the attitudes of Anthony Eden as conforming 'to the cosy and lenitive Butskellism which Conservatives in the '50s persuaded themselves would take all the bother and difficulty out of governing'?* Kedourie came to politics with the benefit of a mordant sense of humour, seldom better deployed than in his account of Richard Crossman's decision, in what Kedourie calls 'the padded cell of the Ministry of Housing', that the Labour Government of 1964 would build 400,000 houses. Why 400,000? Kedourie asks sardonically. 'We may suspect that the only virtue of this figure is that it is a round figure.' But then Harold Wilson, the Prime Minister, got in on the act. It must be 500,000! 'This is it,' said Wilson. 'We'll make housing the most popular single thing this Government does ... That's what I believe in.' That was May. Six weeks later, the Treasury spoke: Fear of the gnomes of Zurich and a run on the pound. No contract whatever was to be signed by any Ministry for three months: 'The Prime Minister wanted to do something which would impress them with our determination to curb incipient inflation.' And so the idiot merry-go-round of unreal projects went on. The style of government described in Crossman's 'Confessions', Kedourie wrote,

* Elie Kedourie, 'Suez Revisited', in *Islam in the Modern World and Other Studies*, London: Mansell, 1980, p. 175.

'sometimes results, no doubt unintentionally, in passages of a Marx Brothers quality.'* It was a pure illustration of rationalism in politics.

In the *Chatham House Version* Kedourie went after rather bigger game: his old *bête noire* Arnold Toynbee, the synoptic historian. In Toynbee he detected signs of a Manichaean passion for pure and undiluted spirituality which entirely rejected the practicalities of politics and the world. Its specific application had been to criticize the British *imperium* in the Middle East up until the middle of the twentieth century as cynical and corrupt. One implication was a Chatham House weakness for Arab nationalism construed as if it were a pure striving for the ideal. Toynbee's 'dogmatic and insistent moralism' led him to admire among modern figures Gandhi, Tolstoy, Lansbury and Sheppard, whom Kedourie characterized as tending 'to the same arid, ineffectual and dogmatic moralism'.** Kedourie had in fact the acute nose of a naturally religious man for bogus spirituality, and brilliantly revealed it in his discussion of the relation between the theosophy of Dag Hammarskjöld and the arrogant pretensions of the United Nations during the 1950s. Kedourie loved poetry, especially that of T. S. Eliot, and on Hammarskjöld quotes the Archbishop's soliloquy from *Murder in the Cathedral*:

> For those who serve the greater cause may
> make the cause serve them,
> Still doing right: and striving with political men
> May make that cause political, not by what they do
> But by what they are.***

In discussing the Suez affair of 1956, Kedourie argued a clear connection between a firm grip on political reality on the one hand, and coherence of will on the other. Nasser's nationalization of the Suez Canal, coming in the early days of the United Nations, generated in many Britons the idea that recourse to force in the pursuit of national interest was both immoral and anachronistic. As Kedourie remarks, 'Manifest in this ideal of a "United Nations Britain" is an intellectual

* Elie Kedourie, *The Crossman Confessions and Other Essays in Politics, History and Religion*, London: Mansell Publishing, 1984, pp. 7–11.

** Elie Kedourie, *The Chatham House Version and other Middle Eastern Studies*, Hanover: University Press of New England, 1984, p. 359.

*** Kedourie, *Islam in the Modern World*, p. 203.

weakness, a wan sentimentality that fails to get a grip on reality. There is here unwillingness to grasp what survival requires in a world from which civility has almost gone, peopled by predators who laugh at the rule of law and take pride and pleasure in brutal flouting of custom and convention.'* And in discussing the hesitations and feebleness of the British government, he remarked: 'It was not a failure of the pound, but failure of will on the part of the Prime Minister which brought the expedition to an end. A man with stronger fibre would have looked the Americans in the eye, called their bluff, and if need be, dared them to choose between the NATO ally and the Egyptian dictator.'**

Like Oakeshott and Letwin, Kedourie was long preoccupied with a certain feebleness in British political action in the early part of the century. It is a major tragedy that he never wrote the book he meditated on this subject. But he did make remarks which suggested what he thought: 'How the pieties that Suez outraged came to strike root, to flourish and luxuriate, how beautiful souls came to set the tone in a public life distinguished not so long ago by some robustness and realism, how scruple decayed into scrupulosity – this remains the central mystery of modern British politics.'***

'Scruple decaying into scrupulosity' is a brilliant formulation of the way in which the Anglo-Saxon world has declined through a collapse in the balance of commonsense categories on which we long relied. Democracy has ceased to be a constitutional category, and been advanced as a comprehensive moral ideal incorporating all the virtues. An ideal justice has come to be invoked (often as 'social justice') in such a way that law-governed and prosperous societies can nevertheless be taken as systematically unjust. Morality has been screwed so tight that only those who speak on behalf of entirely guiltless political entities are to be afforded credit. Sensitivity and good manners were codified and imposed as a form of correct behaviour on whoever could be intimidated. Rationalist monism took many forms, all disruptive of the decencies of tradition. Against this, it is refreshing to read Kedourie echoing Bill Buckley and Patrick Moynihan:

* *Ibid*, p. 190.
** *Ibid*, p. 186.
*** *Ibid*, pp. 190–91.

> De Gaulle, that old sultan, described states as cold monsters. But what saved these monsters from being utterly monstrous was a fierce and touchy sense of honour. The sense of honour has its origins in the pursuit of, and the competition for, power. Involved in it is a jealousy for one's prestige, and a quick readiness to protect it from being damaged – whether by one's own actions or by the actions of others. Based on the pride of power, a sense of honour is, in a Christian or a Kantian scheme, an ambiguous virtue, but it is a virtue all the same. The question is whether, both intelligence and courage failing, an atavistic sense of honour may come to save all these Western states, heavy with undreamt-of prosperity and luxuriating in their feelings of nameless guilt, from passively waiting for the destruction which, if it comes, will surely be in essence self-destruction.*

Shirley Letwin was combative and clear-headed. She was also a charming and accomplished social figure whose active enterprising spirit valuably complemented Oakeshott's social passivity. If Oakeshott was the philosopher in this group, and Kedourie the historian, Letwin could be described as the moralist. In fact, however, each of them covered the entire territory. Letwin was a great reader of novels, and *The Gentleman in Trollope – Individuality and Moral Conduct* is perhaps her most characteristic book. The playwright John Osborne, in an admiring account of it, was most struck by the following remarks:

> In a world of people who think only of getting and spending, who are trying to wipe the slate clean or tie up everything in large, neat sharp-cornered parcels, who confuse authority with power, who shudder at the dappled diversity of the human world, the gentleman will not feel at home . . . When others give in, he may go on fighting . . . He may be a statesman, a farmer, a brewer, a doctor or a parson, but still he will work in the spirit of a potter, shaping and moulding as best he can.**

The key idea here is that of 'the human world' from which Letwin always took her bearings. Her notion of the gentleman was firmly

* Elie Kedourie, 'The United Nations: Hammarskjold and After', in *Islam in the Modern World*, p. 211.
** Diary in the *Spectator*, 14 May 1994.

rooted in English life, and equally firmly disjoined from any notion of rank or status. Indeed, her philosophical transformation of the idea was such that her argument could generate, as a kind of *coup de théâtre*, the implication that the paradigm case of the gentleman in Trollope, the person who most purely expressed this moral type in Trollope's novels, was Madame Max Goestler, a Viennese Jew who married Phineas Finn. To be a gentleman was thus to be a person (of either sex) who orders his or her conduct in appropriate ways. It is not at all, however, an egalitarian conception.

This view led her to defend the English novel of manners against the metaphysical preoccupations of much continental fiction, in which the moral issues of everyday life barely arise. The philosophical counterpart of this contrast was that between the English empirical view of individuality as a developing coherence of desires and obligations on the one hand, and the Platonic disjunction between reason and the passions on the other. Like Popper and other critics of Plato, but in a very different spirit, she took this distinction to underlie the dominant managerialism of modern times. This particular version of Platonism also generated a contempt for the everyday ambitions of ordinary people. She regarded even so sympathetic a figure as de Tocqueville as having just such an aristocratic contempt for ordinariness.

She devoted considerable attention to the idea of law, which she believed to have been extensively corrupted by critical realists and Dworkinian believers in social justice. Human beings lived within a framework of rules constituting law, morals and manners and this framework was sustained by authority and tradition. A common mistake was to confuse authority with power; and again, to confuse the desirability of a project or a law with the authority for it. To this implication of rationalist ways of thinking she attributed the decline of constitutionality in our time.*

In making sense of what came to be called 'Thatcherism' she made use of a characteristically Oakeshottian dialectic. Was Thatcherism a doctrine or ideology, or was it merely a bundle of political expedients? These alternatives, analogous to those between empiricism and ideol-

* See in particular her Bonython Lecture 'Law and Liberty', delivered in Melbourne in 1987, and published by the Centre for Independent Studies (Sydney) in 1987.

ogy which Oakeshott had explored in his famous inaugural lecture 'Political Education' at the London School of Economics, arose, in Letwin's view, from the false belief 'that there are only two ways of conducting politics – either to follow some abstract blueprint or to satisfy the demands of interest groups'.* In fact, Thatcherism must be understood as a contingent response to the political circumstances of Britain in the late twentieth century. In particular, its reference point was a concern for what Letwin called 'the vigorous virtues'. No list, of course, quite captures what is involved here – but she provided one all the same: being upright, adventurous, independent-minded, loyal to friends, and robust against enemies.** The contrast was with such 'softer' virtues as kindness, humility, gentleness, sympathy and cheerfulness.

There is something Aristotelian about this view, and it is Aristotle who reminds us that precision is a function of one's subject matter. In this case, the virtues concretely and therefore confusingly embedded in actual life may be described in a variety of ways, and some are always more fashionable than others. But what had to be emphasized, against a tempting misunderstanding of both the Thatcher government and Letwin's explanation of it, is the mistake of thinking that her moral preoccupations made Thatcher no less a social engineer than the social democrats she opposed. As she herself emphasized, a concern with virtues is formal: 'It is . . . possible for a person to conform to the Thatcherite conception and yet *be* any one of an infinite number of different kinds of person.' To encourage virtues is not to attempt to determine *what* will be done.

What we have here is not an abstract idea of conservatism, but one member of a concrete family of conservative responses to circumstances. It is this settled disposition of mind which, in spite of her general approval of the market, discouraged Letwin from identifying herself unambiguously with the libertarian currents of thought which have so successfully destroyed social democracy in her time. In this she was representative of this particular group of thinkers, for whom asking *how much* government is appropriate was to misunderstand the basic issue of freedom. As she put it in one of the last things she

* Shirley Letwin, *The Anatomy of Thatcherism*, London: HarperCollins, 1992, p. 31.
** *Ibid*, p. 33.

wrote, a talk given to Conservative MP's at the Centre for Policy Studies:

> Conservatives have to explain repeatedly and forcefully that to allow people to run their own lives within a framework of rules maintained by the government is not to encourage jungle warfare but to support free trade, the only civilized way for free people to associate and prosper.*

The issue of market versus planning, or economic versus administrative or managerial considerations, is often important, but can become a species of fundamentalism which conservatives must treat merely as an approximation, for they must not be trapped into believing, wrongly, that every act of government is ipso facto a diminution of the freedom of the citizen.

These remarks arose from looking to a future in which conservatives would find the lines of controversy much more blurred than they had been, and they led Letwin to remark that in 1979 Margaret Thatcher had had (she added 'paradoxically') 'an easy task'. Everything is easy in hindsight, of course. To think about politics is to have a wet finger up there in the wind. What we must now briefly consider is whether there is some general theme which is both relevant to the future and comes from the passage of intellectual history we have been discussing. I think there is.

Oakeshott and those who think like him can certainly offer little practical guidance on policy. They can, however, offer the invaluable gift of intellectual clarity in practical matters. In particular, Oakeshott has analysed with an unparalleled precision the 'poles' between which modern politics has moved, and he has been able to pinpoint one notable error which tends to shipwreck any coherent idea of freedom. He wrote:

> The erroneous belief that all human relationship must be in terms of purposes pursued and actions performed has persuaded many that all human associations must be composed either of persons transactionally related in seeking individual satisfactions, or of persons co-operatively related in seeking common satisfactions, and consequently that the character of a state *must*

* See pp. 177–8.

> be identified as some sort of substantive condition of human circumstance. Thus, a state understood in terms of *societas* is often called 'free enterprise' association, whereas properly speaking it is 'no enterprise' association.*

Freedom for Oakeshott is thus derived from membership of what he calls a 'civil association', a type of relationship constituted by nothing else but subjection to a set of rules. Such an association may be exemplified in that between those who speak a common language. It is only in belonging to an association of this kind that individuals may, by themselves or combining with others, pursue goals which they have freely chosen. Precisely because the State is a compulsory association, it cannot impose upon its subjects any corporate project without in doing so qualifying their freedom, and in practice, of course, modern States have often done just this (especially in war-time). Oakeshott was entirely persuaded that human freedom had been greatly diminished in liberal democracies during his life-time. He was acutely aware of the pressures towards what he occasionally called 'the servile State'.**

A servile State on his view is one that is not ruled by law. Rather, it is *managed* (through instrumental rules masquerading as law) in the pursuit of some overriding purpose such as virtue, welfare, happiness, the satisfaction of human needs, guaranteed security, equality or some other national (and ultimately global) aim. In such a society, as in a despotism, *everything* within the State, including its inhabitants, would become contributory to this aim. The spread of the idea of 'human resources' is one index of the strength of such managerialism in our current view of the world.

I would suggest that the tendency towards an entirely managed world has now become an autonomous movement so embedded in our folklore that it now hardly needs explicit and deliberate advocacy. It enjoys so rich a resource of vocabulary and device as almost to obliterate any alternative way of thinking. It rises in triumph above every failure. This is what Oakeshott meant in judging that rationalism was not only a doctrine but a corruption of thought. It is true that we still *talk* of freedom, and insist that States should be responsive

* Michael Oakeshott, *On Human Conduct*, Oxford: Clarendon Press, 1975, p. 318.
** *Ibid*, p. 301.

to the needs and wants of their subjects, but we do this in the manner of engineers who recognize that there are some rigidities in the construction of an engine which will make it work less rather than more efficiently. Even the theorists of enlightened absolute government in the eighteenth century recognized that certain areas of society worked better if they were not subject to detailed regulation: this, indeed, was the original meaning of the term *laissez-faire*. It was a department of despotic government. On a pessimistic reading of the way we live now, freedom as an ideal now cowers in corners rather contemptuously left vacant by a triumphant managerialism. The end of the Middle Ages has sometimes been understood as the moment when the concept of 'perpetuity' ceased to have any serious meaning. Perhaps we might recognize as a sign of a comparable watershed in our own time the obsolescence of the term 'adventure', for every device of management seeks to guarantee the safety and security of modern populations wherever they might go and whatever they might do. Our world is not only fool-proof; it is also, in its regulatory drive, hero-proof.

The point is to rationalize and manage everything so as to create a system within which human life may be lived as if a human soul were a life-long tourist in this world, a tourist who must be guaranteed a schedule of agreeable experiences. We may illustrate how it works in two spheres: the ideological and the regulatory.

The ideological drive challenges the modern State, an association of individuals living under law, as suffering from systematic defects which effectively negate its unity and render it a set of mutually antagonistic parts. The inventor of this theory was, of course Marx, for whom the antagonistic parts were bourgeois and proletarian. The theory is capable of extensive adaptability, however. The antagonistic parts might be sex, or sexual preference, or race or nation, or indeed anything else that might become current. Each of these 'parts' creates a single compulsory identity (that of worker, or woman, or racial or national culture) which closely circumscribes the possibility of individual enterprise. Workers *essentially* exhibit solidarity with their comrades, women compassion, nationals the spirituality which constitutes their culture, etc. These parts into which the State has been divided are thus suitable entities to be managed in the improved community which is to be constructed.

Ideological management is interesting because it almost caricatures the managerial project. It largely mobilizes the unsophisticated, the 'joiners' of the world. It divides in order to manage. In liberal democratic societies, ideological management has usually been marginal. We are more familiar with regulatory management, the ever increasing tendency of governments, in war or for welfare, to determine how we live, projects usually carried out as ways to give us the gift of empowerment. We might instance the increasing control of education by governments.

This drive to manage society is in our time so pervasive that it has spread beyond the area of political debate and is now enthusiastically carried on, more or less autonomously, by government agencies acting under discretionary powers granted by legislatures which can no longer scrutinize and debate particular issues. In Britain today the problem is dramatized by the mist of regulation coming from membership of the European Community. Even judges, who ought to safeguard us against this tendency, can now be found endorsing it, seeking themselves to exercise managerial power in terms of the interpretation of quite new kinds of rights.

Now what I have briefly sketched will be essentially familiar, and it will seem to bear upon the issue of freedom. But what, it might be asked, is actually *conservative* about anxiety at this development? The answer must be that managerialism profoundly modifies the moral and political character of the British, indeed Anglo-Saxon, and to some extent, more broadly, European, culture we have inherited. For freedom as it features in this argument is not the concern of some party (classical liberals, perhaps) or merely one desirability to be balanced against others. It is the condition without which we cease to be moral beings. And (if I may hazard a moment of pure abstraction) morality is, in a world of galloping socialization, something to which no conservative ought to be indifferent.

APPENDIX

BRITISH CONSERVATISM IN THE 1990s

SHIRLEY LETWIN

It may sound paradoxical but it is nevertheless true that when Mrs Thatcher became Prime Minister in 1979 she had an easy assignment. Not everyone saw things as she did, but no one could deny that Britain was in a sorry state and that something radical had to be done. The Major government was faced with no such obvious assignment.

Then, too, events outside Britain reinforced this blankness. Communism collapsed, the Cold War seemed to be over, and the Labour Party discovered that even so-called democratic socialism would not do. In short, by the time that Major was elected, the late Victorian refrain, 'We are all socialists now', had been replaced by 'We are all capitalists now'. Where does that leave a party and a government which had gained its spurs, at least in recent years, by fighting socialism and communism, by defending capitalism? What was there left to fight? And so we are now entertained by journalists who interlace lines from speeches by Major and Smith to produce what appears to be a single speech which is no less coherent than most political speeches are nowadays. Should we conclude that there is nothing distinctive for a conservative to say or do now?

But before considering that question we should recognize how odd the question is for conservatives especially to be asking. Because of our long exposure to the Cold War abroad and our recent experience of Thatcherism at home we have forgotten something of fundamental importance about British politics and British attitudes, let alone British conservatism. We have forgotten that a state of radical change and violent dispute is not what a British conservative does, or should, consider normal.

The great distinction of Britain is that for many centuries politics has not been the centre of life and even for the handful of dignitaries who happened to hold certain offices. The politicians you meet in Trollope, for instance, are not passionate activists absorbed in great political battles. What makes Trollope's prime minister, Plantagenet Palliser, the Duke of Omnium, so eccentric is that he is miserable unless he is engaged in some great project; his project, however, was hardly one we could consider exciting nowadays – decimal coinage, which was finally introduced not so long ago with barely a ripple. Of course, there have always been issues that divided people and politicians. But the party divisions through most of the nineteenth century were hardly cataclysmic. The Corn Laws were repealed by the Conservatives who had previously favoured them. In one of Trollope's novels, a bill for disestablishing the Church is brought in by the Conservatives, on whom the established Church believed it could always rely, and no one thought the novel outrageous. Members of Parliament hurl insults at each other during the day and dine amicably together in the evening. That was the normal state of politics in Britain until 1945, and in some measure it endured through the 1980s.

It is also true, however, that in the 1980s there was a strong sense of 'going somewhere', of 'so much more to do', as Margaret Thatcher was fond of saying. And no doubt, there was a certain exhilaration, both within and outside the government, because there was so much to be doing and so much was done. Nevertheless, I would like to suggest that the loss of exhilaration is a good thing. It was needed at that time because radical measures had to be introduced. And without the impetus and inspiration provided by a government which had a sense of mission and was led by an indomitable Prime Minister nothing of the sort might have happened. But conservatives ought not to yearn for the constant agitation of a crusade. That frame of mind is suitable for the French, who thrive on revolutions and barricades and constitutional upheavals. In Britain, the ideal, especially among conservatives, has been and should be to make and keep politics unimportant. The job of the government ideally is to keep the ship on an even keel in a calm sea, not to head in and out of typhoons. Of course, changes have always to be introduced – the Reform Acts in the last century were hardly insignificant. But they took effect without producing great traumas, despite the efforts of people like John Stuart Mill to whip up a sense of crisis. Throughout, the British retained their sense of possessing precious liberties and procedures which were well entrenched and secure. The arguments were about policies, about how to keep the ship in good order and afloat, not about abandoning it for another or making an impetuous dash for some distant destination.

In short, the legacy from the Thatcherite years that we might well jettison is the sense of excitement, of a mission to accomplish, of a crusade to join. In doing that, we would be behaving like loyal Thatcherites, for the ultimate, the most profound purpose of the Thatcherite crusade – as many and perhaps even the Prime Minister herself sometimes forgot – was to make such crusades unnecessary. The struggle against Ken Livingstone's monstrous GLC, against the unbelievable activities and profligacy of local councils, against trade unionists' intimidation, against the overmanning and inefficiency of nationalized industries, was a struggle to prevent powerful interest groups from usurping the authority of government and ensuring that the government devoted itself to maintaining a framework of rules and procedures that allowed individuals and voluntary associations to get on with their own projects, without interference by the busy-bodies and bullies in Whitehall, Westminster and Town Halls.

I would suggest then that the Conservative Party should now take the lead in reminding the people of Britain that, thanks to the achievements of the eighties, the kind of politics that they have traditionally preferred, that protects their liberties and allows them to exercise their ingenuity and energy to best advantage, is not the politics of crusade and vituperation. British conservatism does not rely on the vision thing! Instead, Conservatives should take the lead in reminding the people of Britain that they are blessed by a long tradition of living in a parliamentary democracy, the rule of law prevailing so that authority is not usurped by ruthless interest grabbers, native or foreign. Politics is not at the centre of life.

What stands in the way of a return to this British way of politics? One answer is obvious and short: Europe. Nothing in the whole project of creating a European State conforms to the British style of politics. It began with a lie – and I use the word deliberately – when we were asked to vote about entering the Common Market; we were assured that the issue was nothing other than free trade. And now both Sir Edward Heath and Geoffrey Howe assure us that they had made it perfectly clear at the time that we were voting to become a province of a European State. Yet the quotations are not difficult to find – they are all laid out in a pamphlet that the CPS has published. From that lie we proceeded to others. Decisions affecting all of us have been made in a secret conclave by we know not whom; decrees have come pouring in upon us from we know not where. And when the government is asked to explain what it is up to, no one seems to know the answer, or else everyone seems to have or give a different answer. By some strange trick of fate, what might have been a period of calm has become a period of quite remarkable confusion, obfuscation and violent disagreement.

The unfortunate truth is that although 'we are all capitalists now', the battle fought by the Thatcher government has to be fought all over again, but on a new terrain, with a new vocabulary, and new weapons. And what is at issue is even more fundamental than the issue in 1979 – it is the independence of Britain, it is the supremacy of British law and self-government in Britain. But this time we are engaged in what is a more difficult battle because the issues have been camouflaged. Our enemies are well disguised behind more than Birnam Wood.

The Conservative Party has then: 1) to reassert its commitment to a free Britain, and 2) to enter into a variety of agreements and arrangements with her continental neighbours which will not constitute a fortress against her old friend across the Atlantic or against emerging new friends in Eastern Europe. The basic Thatcherite preference for mutually satisfactory agreements among independent agents as the proper way of relating to the rest of the world has to be reasserted on the world stage. What divides M. Delors from the traditional British outlook is that like so many of our continental friends, Delors believes that the only way to secure order is for some central agency to arrange all the bits and pieces in accordance with some overall grand plan – only now we call it 'strategy' which is the social democratic euphemism for socialist planning. Even though 'we are all capitalists now', the Delors of this world still have not grasped the possibility of order that emerges from voluntary transactions among independent agents, made in accordance with rules which dictate only the procedures to be observed and not the substance of the agreements to be reached. The urge to unify, to manage from the centre, to reduce variety to homogeneity has not died with the death of socialism and communism. It has just assumed a new shape. It is a most devious human passion which never disappears because like a chameleon it is so adept at taking on a new form in new circumstances. It turns out, then, that we still have a crusade on our hands; it is the same crusade as in 1979 only more difficult to conduct because so much is vague and confused.

Moreover, we still have to fight the same enemy at home. The urge to centralize, to organize, to submit to experts armed with drawing boards has by no means died within Britain, or even within the Conservative Party. Only now we do it by means of reports. We get a doctor who has been relatively unsuccessful in his profession, who has hardly any experience of the day to day administration of hospitals, especially of centres of excellence, to issue a blue-print for amalgamating this and eliminating that. The excuse is saving the taxpayers money – which is the new way of talking – or 'rationalization', which belongs to the old way of talking. But whatever the words, it is the same old mentality, the same old horror of letting order emerge from the voluntary arrangements made by independent agents. We have by no means lost the old faith in putting our affairs into the hands of those who claim to know what is good for others and how to spend their money for them.

This is not to say that changes should never be made. Of course, hospital facilities or community care may have to be altered. But there are many different ways of making such changes. Issuing reports and imposing them by ministerial decree is the same old socialist methodology in a new guise. Conservatives should address themselves to finding new ways of making such changes.

In addition there is much unfinished work from the Thatcherite era, especially in two fields. One is the welfare state, the other is education. At the IEA, David Green and others have been working to remind us that care for the needy is not necessarily a monopoly of the State, that a variety of voluntary arrangements might do the job better, that such arrangements used to exist and to work, and they were wilfully destroyed. Conservatives should devote themselves to reminding people of the distinction between using the insurance principle and setting up a welfare state to provide for the needy, indeed to emphasize that there are different kinds of needy.

Serious research is wanted to discover the facts about the so-called homeless and single parent families, to break down the old clichés and to think and do something truly original. The NHS reforms need much more explaining, as well as improving; false statistics have to be rebutted. The CPS should be inundated with requests for relevant information and Tory MPs should insist on putting their case and be able to do it effectively instead of letting Jeremy Paxman dominate the discussion.

In education, much remains to be done. Teacher training colleges have yet to be abolished. What is wanted is an energetic, well-informed, persistent campaign against allowing teacher training colleges to brainwash teachers into doing just what is not wanted in order to educate Britain. Again, Tory MPs should have the information at their finger tips and the drive to insist that their criticisms be heard. This is another vital area, which the government has addressed, but far too feebly. And finally, Conservatives need to devote themselves to renewing a great blackspot in Thatcherite reforms, the funding of universities.

It looks as if no one in the government had a clear idea of what the great universities of Britain – no other country has anything like them – are about. What has emerged is an appallingly bureaucratic system which both interferes with the work of universities and has handed power over to the worst elements in the educational bureaucracy. The whole system is rotten – here a real crusade should be launched.

To put it generally, what Conservatives have to do now is to fight off social democracy. That is more difficult than fighting off socialism. For it is easier to make effective speeches against nationalized industries than to fight off the mountain of directives from Brussels or the whispering campaign against privatization. We are constantly being told, though never quite directly, that there is no intrinsic reason for preferring private industry to publicly owned industry by people who swear that they are true blue capitalists. And with this suggestion, we are fed gross misinformation about prices, costs and the regulation of privatized industries. The truth is that privatization, which has never previously happened in the history of the world, is a highly complicated and variegated procedure and most of those who pretend to know about it are in fact ignorant about crucial facts, methods and results. If privatization is to progress, as it should, much more education is needed of and by Tory MPs. Conservatives should stand ready to argue that even if privatized industry were less efficient than nationalized industry it would be preferable because we do not want our government to manage industry or to decide where to build our houses. This is the argument that Thatcherism began to put into practice but has yet to be won. And even though we are all capitalists now we have still to keep reminding people of the virtues of political arrangements that allow for constant change, which permit a great variety of associations invented by energetic, self-moving people who prefer to rely on what they themselves make and choose, people who prefer to take risks instead of live inside a cocoon constructed for them by commissars of Whitehall or town hall.

In connection with town halls, what is wanted is the opposite of the Prime Minister's recent statement suggesting that more powers should be handed over to them. What is wanted is the opposite – liberation from bureaucratic tyrants at the so-called local level is just as essential as at the national level. Indeed the whole concept of local government in Britain is a source of monstrous confusion that needs to be sorted out, for there is no such thing as local government. Since the so-called local government has from the beginning been the womb of socialism, we cannot expect the Labour Party to do this sorting out. Thus clarifying the role of town halls should be an important point on a Conservative MP's agenda and a very difficult one it is, quite apart from the lethal issue of how to fund local authorities.

In short, what Conservatives have to do now is something much less amusing than they had to do in 1979. They have to attend to the details in new proposals. They have to be pedantic and to persuade the public that their pedantry is serving a very important purpose. It remains not just to entrench the achievements of the 1980s, but also to fight off the gross misrepresentations of what was achieved, misrepresentations regularly peddled by the media, especially on television. Conservatives have to explain repeatedly and forcefully that to allow people to run their own lives within a framework of rules maintained by the government is not to encourage jungle warfare but to support free trade, the only civilized way for free people to associate and prosper. It is an exceedingly difficult message to put across, especially in sound bites and all the more so because it has none of the drama associated with a crusade. That is why what we need above all now is a clear and firm understanding of how we want to be governed.

Index

A Proposal to End Inflation, 125n
A Question of Politics, 157n
A Rule to Stabilize the Price Level, 125n
A Treatise of Human Nature, 29n
Acta sanctae sedis, 54
Action Française, 51, 55
Adenauer and the CDU, 55n
Adenauer, Konrad, 59–60
Aflaq, Michel, 130
Alien Powers, 34, 39
Allen, Woody, 31
Amis, Kingsley, 23, 40
Amis, Martin, 23
Anatomy of Thatcherism, The 28, 71, 166n
ANCAP basket, 125
appeasement, 142, 160
Appeasers, The 142n
Aristotle, 103, 167
Astor, Gerald, 34
Athens Declaration, 60
Atlantic Monthly, 150
Atlanticism, 60–1
Attlee government, 160
Australia, monetary issue, 113–14, 117–19, 122–4
Axelrod, Robert, 91

Baker, James, 93
Baldwin, Stanley, 87–8
Bank Charter Acts, 121
Bank of England, establishment of, 116
banking
  central, 121–4, 126–8
  theory, 119–20
Bell, Coral, 148
Bell, Daniel, 15, 82
Benedict, Ruth, 148
Bentham, Jeremy, 157
Bidault, Georges, 49
Birch, 115
Bismarck, Otto, 51
black-marketeers, 92–3
Blackstone, Sir William, 97
Blair, Tony, 67, 76–7
Blood-Dimmed Time, The, 34
Bonython lecture 143, 166n
Bottomley, Virginia, 74
Bourguiba, Habib, 130
Boys from Brazil, The, 26
Brady, Ian, 25
Brezhnev, Leonid, 134
Brzezinski, 146
Buchez, Philippe, 52
Buckley, William F., 14, 164n
Burke, Edmund, 27, 81, 90, 138, 158
Burns, A.R., 113n
Bush, President, 134

Cambridge Review, 154
Campaign for Nuclear Disarmament, 133
capitalism, 63
Carlyle, Thomas, 82
Carr, E.H., 142
Catholic Action movement, 54
Catholicism, 46, 50–6, 59, 61–2, 64–6
Cecil, Hugh, 155
Chamberlain, Neville, 141
change, current preoccupation with, 99–102
chaos theory, 150
Chatham House Version, 163n
Chavez, Linda, 36
China, balance of power and, 148–9
Chirac, President, 78

Chou En-Lai, 130
Christelijke Volkspartij, 59
Christian Democracy, 5
  conservative realism and, 44–67
  development in Europe, 50–6, 66
  European, 48
Christian Democracy in Europe, 49n
Christian Democracy in Italy and West Germany, 50n
Christian Democracy in Western Europe, 49n
Christian Democrats, 46–9, 50
  French, 49, 53–6, 58
  German, 46–8, 50, 55, 57–60
  Italian, 49, 53–60
  politics of, 61
  post war record, 61, 63
Christian Socialism, 52
Christianity, 10–11, 17
Chrysanthemum and the Sword, The, 148
Cicero, 110
Civic Conservatism, 89n
civil association, 169
Clarke, Ken, 47
Clinton administration, 18, 144–5
Cold War, 133–4, 139–40, 142, 144–6, 149–50, 152, 172
Collected Essays, Journalism and Letters, 32
collectivism, 62–4
Coming Anarchy, The, 150
Common Agricultural Policy, 71
Common Market, 174
Commonwealth Bank Notes Act, 114
competition, discipline of, 45
Congress of People's Deputies, 132–4
Conrad, Joseph, 162
Conservatism, 66
Conservatism, 155
Conservatism: foundations and fallacies, 3n
Conservatism
  in the 1990s, British, 172–9
  American, 9–22
  Civic, 89–92
  and cultural identity, 23–43
  the free market and civic, 80–97
  nature of, 44
  neo-, 9, 15–17
  new anxieties, 82–8
  Oakeshott's ideal of, 10–11
  religious, 16–17
  and the State, 74
  touchstone of reality, 160
conservative
  discourse, 151
  realism and christian democracy, 44–67
Conservative Essays 5, 68n, 75n, 78, 79n
Conservative Party, and Christian Democrats, 46–7
Conservative Polical Centre, 48
Conservative Political Thought, 158n
Conservative Realism, the disposition of sceptical faith, 98–111
Conservative realists, three, 154–71
Consumer Price Index (CPI), 122, 125, 127
consumerism, 32
conversation and politics, 102–3
corporativism, 65
Coward, Noel, 33
Cowling, Maurice, 5, 68–9, 78–9
criminals, 25
Cross and the Fasces: Christian Democracy and Fascism in Italy, The 55n
Crossman, Richard, 161
Crossman Confessions and Other Essays, 162n
culture
  adversary and counter-, 86
  links between market and, 96
currencies, domestic, 118–19, 121

Daily Telegraph, 154
Davies, B., 53n
de Gasperi, Alcide, 55, 60
de Gaulle, Charles, 58, 97
de La Tour du Pin, René, 53

de Soto, Hernando, 92
de Tocqueville, Alexis, 166
Delors, Jacques, 67, 175
democracy, 3
  conservative realism and christian, 44–67
  Salvation through, 140–1
  social, 176
Democrazia Cristiana, 60
Denationalization of Money, 116
Distinctiveness of Christian Democracy, 49n
distopianism, 150–1
dollar, Euro, 119, 124
Dowd, Kevin, 124–5
Downing Street Years, The, 120

economic, change and cultural disruption, 82–8
economic issues, USA, 18–19
economics
  free-market, 61–2
  macrostatistics, 20–1
  supply-side, 45
Economist, The, 17
economy
  capitalist, 45
  and welfare, free market, 84
Eden, Anthony, 162
Eleven at Number Ten, 88n
Eliot, T.S., 163
Encounter, 9, 154
End of History and the Last Man, The, 139
Engels, 143
equality, 3
Erhard, Ludwig, 59–60
Ersson, S.O., 49
Esprit movement, 56, 63
Etzioni, A. 154
Eulenspiegel Society, 41–2
Euro-dollar, 119, 124
Europe
  and British conservatism, 174
  and the nation State, 83
European
  idea, 69–70
  integration, 60
European Community, 45
  corruption in, 71
  leaving the, 70–1
European Democracies, 49n
European Democratic Group, 46
European Parliament, 46
European People's Party, 60
European Union, 39, 140
Evans, Ray, 3, 112–28
Evolution of Co-operation, The, 91
Evolution of the Gospel, The 113n
exchange rates, 122–3
Experience of Free Banking, 124n
Experience and its Modes, 160

Fabians, 82
Fairbanks, John, 149
faith, politics of, 104–9
family
  future of the, 83–4
  values, defence of, 61
Fane, George, 112n
Fanfani, Amintore, 56–7
Fascism, 51, 58
federal union, 136
Felix Krull, 38
Feuerbach, 111
Fichte, 159
Financial Times, 84
Firestone, Shulamith, 36
Fogarty, Michael, 49
foreign policy, unrealism and, 129–37
free banking, 125
Free Banking in Britain 117n
Free Banking and Monetary Reform 120n
free market, 86
  and civic Conservatism, 80–97
  economic arguments for, 87
  realism about the, 94–6
free trade, 174
freedom, 169
Freedom and Reality 115n
Friedman, 155
Fukuyama, Francis, 139
Fuller, Timothy, 6, 98–111

Gale, George, 78–9
Gandhi, Mahatma, 130
GATT, 62
Gemelli, Father, 56
genetics, 26
Gentleman in Trollope, The, 37, 85–6, 117, 164
Gilbert, W.S., 26
Gingrich, Newt, 15, 145–6
Giolitti, Giovanni, 54
Glasner, David 120, 121n
gold price rule, 127
gold standard, 115–16, 118, 124–5
Goldsmith, Sir James, 82
Goldwater, Senator, 14–15
Goodhart, Charles, 120n
Gorbachev, Mikhail, 132–4, 139
Gospel of Mammon, 82
government, disintegration of, 130
Graves de communi, 54
Gray, John, 42, 82, 155
Great Depression, 118
Great Melody, A Thematic Biography of Edmund Burke, The, 158
Green, David, 27–8, 176
Greenwood, John, 112n
Gresham, Sir Thomas, 114
Griffiths, Richard, 5–6, 68–79
Gulf War, 144
Gummer, John, 47

Hammarskjöld, Dag, 163
Hanke, Steve, 112n
Hanley, D., 49n
Harmel, Léon, 53
Harries, Owen, 6, 71, 138–52
Hayek, Friedrich von, 13–14, 116, 155
Health Service reforms, 74–6
Heath, Edward, 45–6, 69, 77, 175
Hegel, Georg, 86, 89, 104, 111
Heidenheimer, A.J. 55n
Helsinki Conference (1975), 134
Himmelfarb, Gertrude, 93
Hitler, Adolf, 141–2
Ho Chi Minh, 130
Hobbes, Thomas 27, 104, 107, 161n
Holywell cum Needleworth, 95
homosexuality, 32–3, 38–9, 41–2
Honecker, Erich, 134
Hong Kong, economic success of, 94, 96
Howe, Geoffrey, 175
Hume, David, 24, 29, 92, 120, 157–8
Hunt, David, 45–6, 48, 57
Huntington, Samuel, 152

identity
  American, 34
  central core of, 28–9
  concept of personal, 23–7
  conservatism and cultural, 23–43
  ethnic, 36
  invented, 35–8
  modern theory of, 31
  national, 39–40
  plastic, 41
  social, 27, 37, 41–3
  traditional theory, 27, 33
ideological management, 170–71
ideology and government, 70–6
In Pursuit of Certainty, 82
individualism, 62–4, 84–6
  excessive, 155
  in industry, 80–1
Industrial Revolution, 95
inflation, 114–17, 120–2, 125, 127
  control of, 45
Institute of Economic Affairs, 155
institutions, 89–91
International Institute of Strategic Studies, 148
Islam in the Modern World 163n, 164n
Islamic fundamentalism, 136

Japan, and power politics, 149
Jarman, Lord, 75
Jaruzelski, General, 134
Jefferson, Thomas, 16
John XXIII, 66
Johnson, Dr Samuel, 152
Johnson, Frank, 140
Johnson, President, 160
Jones, David Martin, 150
Judaism, 10–11, 17

Kaiser, Jakob, 59
Kant, Immanuel, 86, 89
Kaplan, Robert, 150
Kedourie
  Elie, 5–6, 39, 86, 89–91, 98, 129, 136, 151
    conservative realist, 154–71
Kenyatta, Jomo, 130
Keynes, John Maynard, 124
Kinnock, Neil, 86
Kirk, Russell, 158
Kissinger, Henry, 139, 144, 146, 149
Koestler, Arthur, 34
Kohl, Chancellor, 47
Kristol, Irving, 5, 9–22
Kulturkampf, 51, 53, 55

Laissez-faire Banking, 124n
Lane, J.-E., 49
Larkin, Philip, 23–4
Lawson, Nigel, 84
League of Nations, 140
Lec, Stanislaw, 140
legal tender, 119
Lenin, 131
Leo XIII, 52–4, 62, 64–5
Letwin
  Shirley, 4, 7, 28, 33, 37, 71–2, 82, 85, 89–91, 98, 112, 117
    conservative realist, 154–71, 172–81
Letwin, William, 27, 33, 155
Leviathan, 161n
Levin, Ira, 26
liberalism, 5, 15–17, 18–20, 81, 156
Lifton, Robert J., 31
Ligue de la Jeune République, 54
Lima, black-market in, 93
Limbaugh, Rush, 20
Lind, Michael, 36
Livingstone, Ken, 173
London: A Social History, 95n
London School of Economics, 11, 153
Longford, Lord, 87–8

Macfarlane, Alan, 95
McGovern, Senator, 14
MacIntyre, Alasdair, 85
MacStiofain, Sean, 38
Maier, Hans, 50n
Major, John, 47, 172
Malcolm, Noel, 5, 44–67
Mann, Thomas, 38
Mao Zedong, 62
Maritain, Jacques, 58, 61, 66
market, Euro-dollar, 119
Marquand, David 47n
Marx, 111, 131, 143
Marxism, collapse of, 81
Marxism Today, 47
Matthew (22:20), 112
media, liberalism and the, 19–20
Menzies, Robert, 140
Michael Oakeshott on Religion, Politics and the Moral Life, 110
Middle East, Russia and the, 129–37
Mill, John Stuart, 157, 174
miners' strike, 84
Minogue, Kenneth, 1–7, 34, 39, 69, 74–5, 78, 138, 154–71
monetary quantities, 120–1
monetary theory, 119–20
Monetary Union, 71
money
  sound (honest), 3, 116–17, 119
  and sovereignty, 112–28
Money and Monetary Policy in Early Times, 113n
monetarism, 72, 120
Monnet, Jean, 58, 60
Montaigne, Michel Eyquem de, 98, 104
Morgenthau, Hans, 140
Moro, Aldo, 60
Motion, Andrew, 23
Mounier, Emmanuel, 56, 61, 63–4, 66
Mouvement Républicain Populaire, 58
Moynihan, Patrick, 164
multiculturalism, 12
multilateralism, 21
Murder in the Cathedral, 163
Murdoch, Rupert, 143

Murri, Don Romolo, 53
Mussolini, Benito, 51, 55–6

National Interest, The, 150
national interests, defence of, 45
National Review, 14
nationalism, 159
Nationalism 39, 86n, 159
Nationalism in Asia and Africa, 154
nativism, 12
NATO, 21, 60, 148
Nehru, Jawaharial, 130
New Yorker, 41
New Zealand, monetary issue, 117, 122–3
New Zealand Reserve Bank Act, 122
Newton, Tony, 47
Next American Nation, The, 36
Niebuhr, Reinhold, 140
Nixon, Richard, 15, 144
Nkrumah, Kwame, 130
Nock, Albert Jay, 14

Oakeshott
  Michael, 3, 5, 6, 9, 13, 16, 22, 68–9, 89–91, 98, 102–11, 117
  conservative realist, 154–71
O'Brien, Connor Cruise, 158
On Being Conservative, 9–10
On the Condition of the Workers, 52
On Human Conduct 158, 169n
Origins of English Individualism, The, 95
Origins of the Second World War, The, 142
Orwell, George, 32
Osborne, John, 165
O'Sullivan, John, 5, 23–43
Other Path, The, 92
Ottoman rule, 129
Oxford Book of Political Anecdotes, 88n
Ozanam, Frederic, 51

Pacem in terris, 66
paedophiles, 42
Parnell, Charles Stewart, 39
parochialism, 23
Parti Démocrate Populaire, 55–6
Partito Popolare, 54–5
patriot, marginal, 38
patriotism, 12
Patten, Chris, 46–7
Paxman, Jeremy, 177
Peel, Sir Robert, 121
perestroika, 132
personalism, 63
philosophy and politics, 102
Pirandello, Luigi, 30
Pius X, 54
Pius XI, 55–7, 62, 64–5
Pius XII, 54
Plato, 102, 166
Policy Review, 27
Political Education (Oakeshott), 109
political theory, realism and, 44
politics
  ideology-ruled, 69
  multicultural power, 152
  and philosophy, 102
  realism and international, 138
Politics of Faction: Christian Democrat Rule in Italy, The, 49n
Politics of Faith and the Politics of Scepticism, The, 104–10
Politics and Society in Western Europe, 49n
populism, 18, 20–1
Porter, Michael, 96
Porter, Roy, 95n
Portrait of an Anti-Semite, 32
Pour une constitution fédérale de l'Europe, 60
Powell, Enoch, 45, 113, 115–16
Power to Change, The, 47n
price stabilization rule, 124–5
Pridham, G., 50n
principle, the perils of, 68–79
prisoner's dilemma, 91
privatization, 73, 80, 177–8
Proclaiming Justice and Peace: Documents from John XXIII to John Paul II, 53n
Prohibition Amendment, 1–2
property
  private, 94–5
  rights, American, 95–6

prosperity, 3
Pryce-Jones, David, 6, 129–37
Public Interest, The, 15
Pursuit of Certainty, The 156n

Quadragesimo anno, 56, 56–7, 62, 64

racism, 23
Rational of Central Banking and the Free Banking Alternative, The, 124n
Rationalism in Politics 9, 13, 68–9n, 102, 157, 159
Rawls, John, 85
Reagan, Ronald, 15, 133
realism
- about markets, 94–6
- attacks against, 139–40, 142–4
- and Christian democracy, conservative, 44–67
- the disposition of sceptical faith, 98–111
- does it have a future?, 138–52
- and horizontal forces, 151

realist discourse, 151
realists, three Conservative, 154–71
Redwood, John, 75
referenda, 19
Reflections on the Revolution in France, 90
Reform Acts, 173
religion, civic, 12–13
religious identity, 26
Rerum Novarum, 52–3
Revolution and Church: The Early History of Christian Democracy, 50n
Reynolds, Alan 112n
Right Ahead: Conservatism and the Social Market, 48n
Riseman, David, 31
Road to Serfdom, The, 14
Roosevelt, Franklin D., 15
Rorty, Richard, 157
Ruhe, Volker, 47–8
rules, modification of, 69
Ruskin, John, 82
Russia
- man-made catastrophe, 130–6
- and the Middle East, 129–37
- post-Cold War, 147–8

St Augustine, 104–6
Salisbury, Lord, 147
SALT and START treaties, 133
Sandel, Michael, 85
Sangnier, Marc, 54, 56
Sartre, Jean-Paul, 32
scepticism, 104–5
Schuman, Robert, 60
Schumpeter, Joseph, 82
Scottish banking, 120–1, 124
secularism, 17, 19
seigniorage, 113–14
Selected Writings, 82n
Selgin, George, 125–6
sexism, 23
sexuality, 26
Significato del corporativismo, 56
Sillon movement, 54, 56
silver standard, 118
Smith, Adam, 13, 120–1
Smith, Vera C., 124n
social
- class, 26–7
- conflict, 41–3
- conventions, 91–3
- democracy, 177
- justice, 3, 51
- market economy, 59
- policy and the mentally ill, 89–90
- solidarity, 59

Social Democrats, 59
Social and Political Movements in Western Europe, 50n
socialism, 14, 62
Socrates, 102, 104–6, 111
sovereign risk, 116
sovereignty, 138
- and money, 112–28

Stalin, Joseph, 62, 132–3, 135
Star Wars, 133
State
- authority of the, 117–19
- servile, 169

statism, 15–17, 19
Stephenson, John, 38
sterling, pound, 118–19
Strauss, Leo, 16
Sturzo, Don Luigi, 54–5
Suez Revisted, 162n
systematization, 98

Taylor, A.J.P., 142
Taylor, Charles, 85
Thatcher, Margaret, 45–7, 71–3, 77, 81, 120, 133, 155, 172–3
Thatcherism, 71–3, 166–8, 172, 174, 178
The Me Decade, 31
Theory of Justice, 85
Thomism, 66
Thorneycroft, Peter, 115
Thucydides, 139
Timberlake, Richard, 112n
Times Literary Supplement, 154
Tomlinson Report, 75
Toniolo, Giuseppe, 53, 56, 65
Toryism, One Nation, 45
totalitarianism, 156
Toynbee, Arnold, 163
trade union reforms, 63
tradition and change, 101
transsexualism, 36
Treatise of Human Nature, 92
Trilling, Lionel, 82, 86
tripolar conceptualization, 148
triumphalism, 80
Trollope, Anthony, 117–19, 166, 172
Twenty Years' Crisis, The, 142

United Nations, 21, 140
unrealism and foreign policy, 129–37
USA
  American national identity, 34–7, 40
  conservatism, 9–22
  'deaf community', 41
  Democratic Party, 15, 21
  economic issues, 18–19
  monetary issue, 114–15, 118–19, 122
  post-Cold War, 144–5
  Republican Party, 13–15, 20–1
  school board politics, 18–19
  and Soviet expansion, 133
utopianism, 144

van Keesbergen, K. 49n, 50n
Vocabulary of Politics, The, 157
von Papen, 57

Walsh, M., 53n
Walters, Sir Alan, 81, 112
Wealth of Nations, The 121n
Webb, Beatrice, 157
Weber, Max, 13
Webster, R.A., 55n
Weldon, T.D., 157
welfare state, 176–7
  and free market economy, 84
Which Kind of Monetary Policy, If Any?, 121n
White, Laurence 117, 121n
Wight, Martin, 139
Wildavsky, Aaron, 41
Willetts, David, 6, 80–97
Wilson, Harold, 68–9, 76, 161
Wilson, James Q., 30
Wittgenstein, Ludwig, 7
Wolfe, Tom, 31
Wood, John, 115
World Bank, 147
Wriston, Walter, 147

Yeager, Leland, 122
Yeltsin, Boris, 132–6

Zentrum party, 51, 55
Zuckerman, A.S. 49n